Choosing The Right Marriage Partner

Kinds of people you should not rush to marry

Archbishop Nicholas Duncan-Williams

Copyright © 2024 by Archbishop Nicholas Duncan-Williams. All rights reserved. No part of this book may be reproduced in any form or by any electronic or mechanical means, including information storage and retrieval systems, without written permission from the author, except for the use of brief quotations in a book review.

Amplified Bible, Classic Edition (AMPC) Copyright © 1987 by The Lockman Foundation.

King James Version (KJV) Public Domain.

New King James Version (NKJV) Scripture taken from the New King James Version®. Copyright © 1982 by Thomas Nelson. Used by permission. All rights reserved.

New International Version (NIV) Holy Bible, New International Version®, NIV® Copyright ©1973, 1978, 1984, 2011 by Biblica, Inc.® Used by permission. All rights reserved worldwide.

Editorial Director: David Ljunggren -- www.ministryscribe.com

***In some instances, there may be an open quote without a closed quote, a capital in mid-sentence, or other grammatical irregularities. That is due to the exact copying of the version and not a mistake or oversight.

The saddest conflict of destiny is when two good people who were never meant to marry, do so.

In the sacred garden of a godly union,
Two hearts entwine, in divine communion.
Rooted in faith, their love does flourish,
Nurtured by grace, it's destined to nourish.

A covenant made, under watchful skies,
Promises exchanged, with no disguise.
God at the center, their steadfast guide,
Through storms and sunshine, always by their side.

Like trees planted by rivers of water,
Their love grows stronger, never to falter.
Leaves may wither, but their roots run deep,
In God's love, their harvest they reap.

Patience and kindness, the fabric of their days,
Forgiveness and mercy, in all their ways.
Selflessly serving, with hearts wide open,
Speaking truth in love, with words softly spoken.

In the dance of life, they move as one,
Under the moon, and under the sun.

Hand in hand, facing whatever comes,
With God's grace, all challenges overcome.

A beacon of hope, for all to see,
A testament of what love ought to be.
Reflecting God's love, in every action,
Their marriage, a divine attraction.

Through years that pass, their love does prove,
That Godly marriages, surely move
Mountains of doubt, and seas of fear,
With faith as their anchor, God always near.

So here's to the lovers, in God they trust,
Building a legacy, from new birth to dust.
In the realm of the celestial, their love does shine,
A godly marriage, both timeless and divine.

- Author Unknown

Contents

Preface	ix
Introduction	xiii
1. Making a Good Choice	1
Red Flags for Women	17
2. Don't Rush to Marry a Nabal	18
3. Don't Rush to Marry an Amnon	31
4. Don't Rush To Marry An Ahab	42
5. Don't Rush to Marry a Solomon	53
Red Flags for Men	63
6. Don't Rush To Marry A Jezebel	64
7. Don't Rush To Marry A Delilah	77
8. Don't Rush to Marry Lot's Wife	88
9. Don't Rush to Marry a Potiphar's Wife	101
10. Don't Rush To Marry A Michal	113
Epilogue	123
About the Author	127

Preface

At the heart of a search for a godly spouse lies the profound strength of prayer and the immutable authority of God's Word. It is here we commence our journey. Acknowledging the beautiful alignment between your desires and God's will, approach His presence with confidence and specificity, ready to claim His promises for your life. In this process, intentionally superimpose God's Word upon the crucial decision of selecting a marriage partner by declaring the following:

> *I declare and superimpose the Word of God according to Genesis 2:18, affirming that 'It is not good that the man should be alone; I will make him a helper suitable for him.' (NIV) I believe and declare that God is actively preparing a suitable partner for me, one who complements and supports God's purpose in my life. I am not meant to journey through life alone, and I trust in God's perfect timing to reveal His choice of a marriage partner for me.*

Preface

I proclaim the truth of Isaiah 62:4-7 over my life, declaring, 'Thou shalt no more be termed Forsaken...for the Lord delighteth in thee.' I declare that God delights in my future marriage, orchestrating godly connections that lead to a joyous union. I refuse to be labeled forsaken or desolate; instead, I am called Hephzibah, for my land shall be married. I commit to persistent prayer, giving God no rest until He establishes my marital destiny and makes my relationship a glory to His name.

By the authority of Ecclesiastes 4:9-12, I declare, 'Two are better than one...and a threefold cord is not quickly broken.' I declare the strength and support that come from a godly partnership and invite God to be the center of my future marriage. I declare that my future spouse and I will lift each other up in times of trouble, provide warmth and companionship to one another, and stand united against any challenge by the strength of our threefold cord.

I stand on the promise of 2 Timothy 4:18, declaring, 'And the Lord shall deliver me from every evil work, and will preserve me unto his heavenly kingdom.' (KJV) I declare God's protective hand over my journey toward marriage, believing He will shield me from harmful relationships and preserve me for a marriage that glorifies Him. I trust in His sovereign protection and guidance, leading me to a partner with whom I can fulfill His heavenly kingdom's purposes.

With the victory of Colossians 2:14-15, I declare, 'Blotting out the handwriting of ordinances that was against us...triumphing over them in it.' I renounce any spiritual obstacles or hindrances to God's plan for my marriage. Through the victory of the cross, I declare freedom from any generational curses, negative patterns, or enemy schemes that would oppose my godly *union. I walk in victory and freedom, expecting God's best for my marriage.*

By speaking these declarations, you align your heart with God's Word, standing in faith for a godly marriage partner. Through the power of declaration, you invite God's will to manifest in your life, trusting in His promises to guide you into a relationship that honors Him and fulfills His purpose.

Introduction

Do not be unequally-yoked with unbelievers. For what fellowship has righteousness with lawlessness? And what communion has light with darkness? And what accord has the Christ with Belial? Or what part has a believer with an unbeliever? And what agreement has the temple of God with idols? For you are the temple of the living God. And God has said: I will dwell in them and I will walk among them. I will be their God and they shall be my people.

— 2 Corinthians 6:14-16 (KJV)

Choosing the right marriage partner is not merely important—it is the bedrock upon which a fulfilling and enduring union is built. The gravity of this decision cannot be overstated, for it influences not only the lives of two individuals but also the fabric of communities and generations to come.

Yet, in a world where the heart's desires often cloud judgment, distinguishing between a good person and the right person for marriage emerges as a pivotal discernment. This differentiation is subtle yet profound, for compatibility transcends mere goodness, embedding itself in the areas of destiny, purpose, and divine alignment.

The journey towards finding a life partner is fraught with misconceptions and fairy-tale ideals that seldom withstand the tests of real life. A person may embody kindness, generosity, and integrity yet not align with another's soul in the dance of lifelong partnership. This distinction is crucial, for it acknowledges that while everyone is potentially a good person, not everyone can fulfill the role of the right person for you. It invites us to look beyond the surface, to discern not just the heart but also the harmony of paths, the convergence of destinies, and the alignment of life's calling.

Marriage, as ordained by God, is a union unlike any other, where the spiritual, emotional, and practical dimensions of life intertwine. It is not merely a contract or a societal arrangement but a covenant that mirrors Christ's commitment to the Church. This divine institution, however, is navigated by imperfect beings tasked with the challenge of forging a life together despite their flaws and differences. The notion that any two Christians can marry and thrive merely by virtue of their faith oversimplifies the complexity of human relationships and the unique dynamics of marital life. It overlooks the essential role of compatibility, mutual respect, and shared vision in sustaining a marriage.

At the heart of every Christian is the ongoing process of transformation, a journey from glory to glory, where the likeness of Christ is being formed within us. Yet, this divine work does

Introduction

not erase our human nature overnight. We remain beings of flesh and blood, carrying our flaws, our pasts, and our unique personalities into every relationship. Acknowledging this human element is vital, for it allows us to extend grace to ourselves and our partners, understanding that growth is a journey shared, not a destination reached alone.

This book emerges as a beacon for those navigating the waters of potential marriage, aiming to illuminate the path with wisdom gleaned from Scripture, experience, and the Holy Spirit's guidance. It ventures beyond the conventional advice on finding a good partner, delving into the crucial conversation about avoiding potential pitfalls that could derail a marriage before it even begins. By examining the lives of biblical characters, we uncover timeless lessons on compatibility, character, and the consequences of ignoring red flags.

The stories of biblical characters offer a treasure trove of insights into human nature, divine grace, and the complexities of relationships. By revisiting these familiar narratives with a focus on their implications for marriage, we gain a deeper understanding of the traits that foster harmony and those that sow discord. These narratives, rich with historical and spiritual significance, serve as mirrors reflecting the timeless challenges and triumphs of marital life.

One of the most daunting aspects of relationships is recognizing that not all are meant to culminate in marriage. The ability to walk away from a partnership that, despite its potential for happiness, may lead to long-term suffering requires immense courage and faith. This book seeks to empower readers with the wisdom to identify when a relationship, however

Introduction

promising it may seem, could hinder their ability to fulfill God's purpose for their lives.

In the quest for a life partner, the role of the Holy Spirit cannot be overstated. Beyond the wisdom contained in these pages lies the deeper, more profound guidance of the Spirit, who illuminates the path, comforts the heart, and confirms the soul's deepest truths. It is this divine companionship that ensures the journey towards marriage is not walked alone but hand in hand with the One who knows our end from our beginning.

As you embark on this journey of discernment, may you find within these pages not just guidance but also hope and encouragement. The path to finding a marriage partner is as unique as the individuals walking it, filled with moments of joy, revelation, and growth. Welcome to a world where marriages are not just endured but enjoyed, where wisdom paves the way to love's true fulfillment.

Before we move to Chapter 1, let me offer a simple prayer for you.

Dear Heavenly Father, Guide the readers of this book with Your wisdom and light. Help them discern the qualities of a godly partner, strengthen them to wait on Your timing, and prepare their hearts for a marriage that glorifies You. Bless their journey towards love and partnership, enveloped in Your grace and truth. In the name of Jesus. Amen.

Chapter 1

Making a Good Choice

A successful marriage is always a triangle: a man, a woman, and God.

— Cecil Myers

The journey toward marriage is as old as humanity, yet the pathways to this sacred union vary significantly across different cultures and societies. In the grand myriad of human relationships, choosing whether—and whom—to marry is one of the most significant decisions an individual can make. This decision, steeped in personal, familial, and societal expectations, transcends mere preference to touch the very core of our existence.

In many cultures, arranged marriages have long been the norm, where families play a pivotal role in selecting a spouse, often intending to strengthen familial bonds or economic ties. In these contexts, the individual's choice may be secondary to broader considerations, a nod to traditions that have guided generations. Conversely, in societies where personal autonomy and romantic love are highly valued, the decision to marry and the choice of a partner rests mainly in the hands of the individuals involved.

Yet, even within these frameworks of apparent freedom, societal and familial pressures can exert a profound influence. From subtle suggestions to explicit expectations, the voices of family and community often resonate in the background of one's decision-making process. The pressure to marry by a certain age, to find a partner who aligns with specific societal standards, or even to choose someone within a specific social, economic, or political class can be overwhelming.

Acknowledging these diverse contexts is crucial, for it frames the choice of a marriage partner not as a straightforward decision but as a complex interplay of personal desires, cultural norms, and spiritual convictions. Despite the myriad influences shaping this decision, the fundamental principle remains: the choice to marry and the selection of a partner are profoundly personal decisions that have significant implications for one's future happiness and spiritual growth.

This chapter seeks to underscore the importance of personal decision-making in choosing a marriage partner. It is a call to navigate the waters of cultural expectations, societal pressures, and familial advice with a heart tuned to God's guidance and a mind informed by wise counsel. For at the heart of the choice to marry lies the opportunity to build a life with someone who not only complements and challenges you but also shares your deepest values and aspirations.

As we delve into the intricacies of making a good choice, we hold onto the belief that, with thoughtful consideration and godly guidance, it is possible to choose a partner with whom a fulfilling, God-honoring marriage can be built.

This journey begins with understanding the concept of choice in marriage, acknowledging the variety of cultural contexts, and highlighting the paramount importance of personal decision-making despite societal or family pressures. In doing so, we set the stage for a deeper exploration of what it means to make a good choice in selecting a life partner for the sacred covenant of marriage.

What is the Right Choice?

In the quest for a marriage partner, the distinction between choosing a "good person" and the "right person" is paramount. A good person, by general standards, exhibits universally admired qualities: kindness, integrity, and generosity.

However, the right person for marriage transcends these admirable traits, aligning more deeply with one's personal values, life goals, and spiritual beliefs. This alignment fosters a relationship where both partners can thrive, not just as individuals but as a united force navigating the complexities of life together.

The right choice in a marriage partner is someone with whom you share profound compatibility, not only in interests but in core aspects of life such as values, vision for the future, and notions of family and commitment. This person encourages mutual growth, challenging and supporting you to evolve into your best self while you reciprocate in kind.

With the right person, you can fully be yourself—your true,

unguarded self—without fear of judgment or rejection. This level of acceptance and understanding is the fertile ground in which love can grow and flourish over a lifetime.

The Importance of Making the Right Choice

Choosing the right partner is crucial for establishing a foundation of emotional stability and mutual support. A harmonious home environment, where love and respect reign, is often the result of two people making a conscious decision to journey through life together as partners who are well-matched in the most critical aspects of their lives.

Consider the story of Sarah and Paul, a couple who exemplify the positive outcomes of making the right choice. Sarah, a strong believer with a passion for humanitarian work, and Paul, equally committed to his faith and service to others, met during a mission trip. Their shared values and mutual respect for each other's aspirations created a strong bond between them.

Throughout their marriage, they have faced challenges, from financial hardships to decisions about family planning, but their aligned visions for life and unwavering support for one another have turned potential obstacles into opportunities for growth. Their home is a testament to the peace and joy that come from a partnership based on deep compatibility and mutual encouragement.

Another scenario highlighting the importance of the right choice involves Thomas and Mary. Thomas, an artist with a free spirit, and Mary, a teacher with a love for structure and stability, might have seemed mismatched at first glance.

However, their underlying compatibility in core values,

such as their commitment to God and a shared belief in the importance of kindness and compassion, has allowed them to build a life together where their differences are not points of contention but sources of enrichment. Their ability to be themselves, fully and fearlessly, has nurtured a relationship marked by creativity, laughter, and an unbreakable bond.

These stories underscore that the right choice in a marriage partner is not about finding someone perfect but about finding someone with whom you can navigate life's imperfections with grace, love, and mutual respect. The benefits of such a choice are immeasurable, affecting not just the couple but everyone around them, from their children and families to their communities. A marriage built on the foundation of the right choice is a beacon of light, a testament to the power of love guided by wisdom and intentionality.

Contexts for Finding the Right Spouse

Finding a spouse who aligns with one's deepest values and beliefs often begins in environments that reflect those very principles. For a child of God, the church serves as fertile ground for meeting potential partners who share a commitment to faith. By its nature, this setting fosters a sense of community, shared purpose, and spiritual growth, making it ideal for forming deep, meaningful connections.

Church activities, such as Bible study groups, volunteer work, and fellowship gatherings, provide opportunities to observe individuals in settings that reveal their character and values. In these contexts, one can see how a person interacts within a community, how they serve others, and how they live out their faith in daily life.

However, it's crucial to approach these settings with the right mindset. While church and community activities can be wonderful places to meet a potential spouse, they should not be viewed purely as matchmaking venues. Instead, participation should be driven by a genuine interest in the church activity or service itself, with openness to the possibility of a relationship developing naturally. This approach ensures that any connection is based on shared values and genuine compatibility rather than a contrived effort to find a partner.

Essential Qualities to Look for in a Future Spouse

In discerning the right choice for a marriage partner, certain qualities stand out as indicators of a strong, healthy, and spiritually grounded individual. These qualities go beyond surface-level attributes to touch on a person's character and approach to life and relationships.

Treatment of Others: Observe how they interact with people in various situations, especially those in vulnerable positions. A potential spouse's true character is often revealed in their kindness, patience, and respect for others, echoing the biblical call to "love your neighbor as yourself" (Mark 12:31).

Financial Management Habits: Financial stewardship is a critical aspect of a life shared together. Look for someone who demonstrates wisdom and responsibility in managing resources, reflecting the biblical principle of stewardship found in Luke 16:11, *"So if you have not been trustworthy* *in handling worldly wealth, who will trust you with true riches?"* (*NIV*)

Reactions to Stressful Situations: Life is replete with challenges, and a person's response to stress can reveal much about their character. Seek a partner who approaches difficulties with patience, resilience, and faith, embodying the peace that Philippians 4:7 describes as *"the peace of God, which transcends all understanding, will guard your hearts and your minds in Christ Jesus."* (NIV)

How They Treat You Publicly and Privately

In addition to observing how a potential spouse interacts with others and manages life's stresses and finances, it's equally important to consider how they treat you both in public and private settings. The dynamics of your interactions can offer profound insights into the nature of your relationship and your potential partner's character.

How a person treats you, especially during moments of disagreement or when you fail to meet their expectations, can reveal much about their respect for you and their capacity for empathy and understanding. In public, does your partner support you and handle disagreements gracefully, or do they belittle and embarrass you? Privately, are they patient and kind, or dismissive and critical? These behaviors are indicative of their true nature and how they value the relationship.

It's essential to assess whether your partner can accept constructive feedback without becoming defensive or moody. A relationship thrives on the ability of both partners to communicate openly, accept correction, and work together toward improvement. This dynamic of mutual respect and the willingness to grow together is crucial for a healthy, enduring marriage.

Maya Angelou wisely stated, "When people show you who they are, believe them the first time." This advice is particularly relevant in the context of choosing a life partner. Early in the relationship, individuals often present their best selves, yet their reactions to stressful situations or disagreements can unveil their true character. If these initial indicators raise concerns, it's important to take them seriously. While people can change and grow, fundamental aspects of their character and how they treat those closest to them tend to remain consistent over time.

The treatment you receive from a potential spouse, both in public and in private, offers a window into the future of your relationship. It speaks to the respect, love, and kindness you can expect to give and receive throughout your life together. As you navigate the journey of finding the right spouse, let these insights guide you toward a partner who not only shares your values and life goals but also treats you with the dignity and love you deserve.

Observing Behavior in Various Situations

One of the most telling ways to discern the character of a potential marriage partner is by observing their behavior across a range of situations. People's true colors often shine through not in moments of ease and comfort but in times of challenge and stress or when they are unaware that they are being observed.

For instance, a person's treatment of service workers—waiters, cleaners, retail employees—can be incredibly revealing. Respect and kindness toward individuals in service roles demonstrate empathy, humility, and an understanding of equality that is crucial for a healthy relationship.

Consider the case of Jonathan and Lisa. While dining out, Jonathan's polite interaction with a waiter who mixed up their order showcased his patience and kindness. Lisa observed not only his words but also his demeanor, which was devoid of condescension or impatience. This small, everyday interaction spoke volumes to Lisa about Jonathan's respect for others, regardless of their job or status.

Financial stability can fluctuate, and how a person manages these ups and downs is critical. Observing someone during a period of financial abundance is as important as seeing how they handle scarcity. James, for example, became more generous and involved in church work when he received a promotion, illustrating his belief in sharing blessings. Conversely, when Ruth faced a job loss, her resilience and refusal to let stress dominate her interactions with her partner highlighted her strength of character and trust in their partnership.

As we have seen, how a potential partner treats you in different settings can offer insights into the depth of their respect and affection for you. Consistency in treatment, whether in public or private, signifies a genuine regard for you. Take the story of Deborah and Alexander. Deborah noticed that Alexander was as attentive and respectful to her in front of his friends as when alone. This consistency reassured Deborah of Alexander's sincerity and the importance he placed on their relationship.

Martha and John's relationship clearly shows the importance of observing behavior in various situations. Martha noted John's respectful attitude toward their elderly neighbor, his calmness during a stressful house move, and his consistent support for her career ambitions, whether in private discussions or at social gatherings. These observations confirmed to Martha that John possessed the empathy, resilience, and respect she valued in a life partner.

Observing a potential spouse's behavior in these varied scenarios allows for a comprehensive understanding of their character. The accumulation of these small, everyday moments builds the foundation for a relationship grounded in mutual respect, shared values, and enduring love.

The Reality of Love and Rational Decision Making

The adage "love is blind" has often been cited to justify overlooking potential issues in a relationship, suggesting that love can conquer all without the need for scrutiny or judgment. However, this notion does a disservice to the complexity and depth of true love.

Real love, especially in the context of choosing a life partner for marriage, is not blind but perceptive. It sees clearly, understands deeply, and chooses wisely. It is a love that recognizes and appreciates the fullness of the other person, including their strengths and flaws, and makes a conscious, informed decision to commit.

Critical thinking during courtship is not about cynicism or looking for flaws for the sake of it but about observing and evaluating how well-suited you are to each other. It's about asking important questions: Do our values align? Can we support each other's dreams and ambitions? How do we handle conflict? It involves being honest with oneself about what is truly important in a partner and being vigilant about red flags that could indicate potential problems in the future.

Recognizing and Interpreting Red Flags

A red flag in the context of choosing a marriage partner refers to any behavior, trait, or situation that raises concerns about the suitability of a potential spouse. These warnings are indicators that something may not be right and warrant closer attention. Red flags can range from inconsistencies in behavior and lack of respect for boundaries to serious issues like dishonesty or manipulative behavior.

The importance of heeding these warnings cannot be overstated. Ignoring red flags can lead to significant challenges in a marriage, from minor irritations to fundamental disagreements that could jeopardize the relationship's stability. Recognizing these signs early on allows one to address potential issues before they become entrenched patterns.

Here are some specific red flags to be aware of:

Lack of Respect: Respect is foundational to any relationship. A potential partner who disrespects you, others, or themselves can be a significant red flag. This can manifest as belittling comments, disregard for boundaries, or consistent rudeness. Proverbs 22:10 advises, "Drive out the mocker, and out goes strife; quarrels and insults are ended," (NIV) highlighting the discord that disrespect can bring.

Poor Financial Management: A partner who exhibits irresponsible financial behavior, such as excessive spending without regard for future needs or an unwillingness to contribute to mutual financial goals, can be a cause for concern. 1 Timothy 5:8 warns, "Anyone who does not provide for their relatives, and especially for their own household, has denied the faith and is worse than an unbeliever," (NIV) emphasizing the importance of responsible stewardship.

Unwillingness to Grow: A relationship cannot thrive without growth. Suppose a partner is unwilling to learn, change, or grow spiritually, emotionally, or intellectually. In that case, it can hinder the growth of the relationship. 2 Peter 3:18 encourages believers to "grow in the grace and knowledge of our Lord and Savior Jesus Christ." (NIV) Growth is a vital component of a Christian life and, by extension, a Christian marriage.

Practical Steps for Avoiding the Wrong Choice

Recognizing red flags is the first step; responding to them appropriately is crucial for ensuring that you make wise decisions regarding your relationships.

Seek Counsel: Do not hesitate to seek the wisdom of trusted mentors, counselors, or pastors when red flags arise. They can offer objective advice and guidance based on their experience and understanding of biblical principles. Proverbs 15:22 states, *"Plans fail for lack of counsel, but with many advisers, they succeed,"* (NIV) underscoring the value of wise counsel in making important decisions.

Prayer: Bring your concerns to God in prayer, asking for clarity, wisdom, and guidance. James 1:5 promises, *"If any of you lacks wisdom, you should ask God, who gives generously to all without finding fault, and it will be given to you."* (NIV) Prayer is a source of comfort and direction when facing difficult decisions about a relationship.

Community and Spiritual Guidance: Lean on your church for support and guidance. Fellow believers can provide spiritual insight and practical advice, helping you to see your situation from a broader perspective. Galatians 6:2 encourages us to *"Carry each other's burdens, and in this way, you will fulfill the law of Christ."* (NIV) The support and guidance of a community grounded in faith can be invaluable.

Consider Ending the Relationship: If, after careful consideration, prayer, and counsel, the red flags continue to raise significant concerns, it may be necessary to consider ending the relationship. While this decision is never easy, it is sometimes the best course of action for both individuals' spiritual and emotional well-being.

Making decisions about relationships is complex and challenging, but by paying attention to red flags, seeking God's guidance, and leaning on the wisdom of the community, you can navigate these waters with greater confidence and clarity, ultimately making choices that honor God and promote your best interests.

Questions for Self-Reflection and Discussion

Choosing a life partner is among the most significant decisions you will make. It requires not just the heart's involvement but the mind's discerning judgment. Here are several reflective questions designed to help you think deeply about your relationship and potential partner to aid in this critical evaluation. These questions can serve as a guide for personal journaling or as discussion points with a trusted advisor, mentor, or close friend.

Values and Beliefs: Do my partner's core values and beliefs align with mine? How do our spiritual beliefs converge or diverge, and how could this impact our future together?

Life Goals and Ambitions: Are our life goals and ambitions compatible? Can we support each other in achieving these goals without sacrificing our own dreams?

Conflict Resolution: How do we handle disagreements? Are we able to discuss issues openly and respectfully, or do conflicts lead to avoidance or escalation?

Family Dynamics: How does my partner interact with their family and mine? What role do we envision for our families in our life together?

Financial Management: What are our attitudes towards money and financial management? Do we have similar strategies for saving, spending, and investing?

Leisure and Interests: Do we enjoy spending time together, and how do we manage differences in interests? Can we respect and support each other's hobbies and leisure activities?

Communication Style: How effectively do we communicate? Are we able to share our thoughts, feelings, and concerns openly?

Adaptability and Growth: How does my partner respond to change or challenges? Are they open to growth and self-improvement?

Treatment of Others: How does my partner treat people they are not trying to impress? Do they show kindness and respect to everyone, regardless of status or relationship?

Red Flags: Have I noticed any red flags or behaviors that concern me? How have I addressed these concerns, and what was the outcome?

Mutual Respect and Support: Do I feel respected, supported, and valued in this relationship? Do I offer my partner the same level of respect, support, and value?

Future Vision: How do we envision our future together? Do our ideas of a happy life align, and how do we plan to navigate differences?

Trust and Security: Do I feel emotionally secure and trusted in this relationship? Are there any trust issues, and if so, what are their roots?

Personal Space and Independence: How do we balance our time together with our need for individual space and independence?

Handling of Stress and Adversity: How does my partner react under stress or when faced with adversity? Does it align with how I manage stress and challenges?

Journaling your thoughts in response to these questions or discussing them with someone you trust can provide valuable insights into your relationship. This reflective process is not meant to judge but to deepen your understanding of your partnership's dynamics and the potential for a shared future. Remember, the goal is to build a foundation for a relationship that is not just enduring but enriching and fulfilling for both partners.

Red Flags for Women

Chapter 2

Don't Rush to Marry a Nabal

The greatest marriages are built on teamwork, a mutual respect, a healthy dose of admiration, and a never-ending portion of love and grace.

— Fawn Weaver

Wisdom and discernment are indispensable companions in the journey toward finding a life partner. Often, we encounter individuals who, at first glance, seem to embody the qualities we desire in a spouse. However, beneath the surface, traits may lie detrimental to a healthy, godly marriage. These warning signs, or "red flags," are crucial to recognize and understand.

Among the myriad of examples in Scripture that guide us in making wise relationship decisions, the account of Nabal stands out as a stark reminder. His story serves not only as a historical record but also as a case study of the dangers of entangling oneself with a person characterized by folly and disregard for godliness.

The narrative of Nabal and David, found in 1 Samuel 25, unfolds during a tumultuous period in David's life. David, who would later become the king of Israel, was at this time fleeing from King Saul's jealous wrath. In his wanderings, David and his men protected the shepherds of a wealthy man named Nabal, who owned vast flocks and herds in the region of Carmel.

Nabal, whose name poignantly means "fool" in Hebrew, lived up to his namesake through his actions and attitudes. Despite David's respectful request for provisions—a request made in light of the protection he had afforded Nabal's shepherds—Nabal's response was churlish and dismissive.

> "Then Nabal answered David's servants, and said, 'Who is David, and who is the son of Jesse? There are many servants nowadays who break away each one from his master. Shall I then take my bread and my water and my meat that I have killed for my shearers, and give it to men when I do not know where they are from?'" 1 Samuel 25:10-11 (NKJV).

David's reaction to Nabal's refusal reveals the gravity of the insult as he prepares to avenge the slight against his men and himself. However, the narrative takes a pivotal turn with the intervention of Abigail, Nabal's discerning and wise wife. Recognizing the impending danger, she swiftly acts to make amends, bringing provisions to David and pleading for peace. Her actions avert disaster and highlight her as a figure of wisdom and grace in stark contrast to her husband's folly.

> "Now when Abigail saw David, she dismounted quickly from the donkey, fell on her face before David, and bowed down to the ground. So she fell at his feet and said: 'On me, my lord, on me let this iniquity be! And please let your maidservant speak in your ears, and hear the words of your maidservant. Please, let not my lord regard this scoundrel Nabal. For as his name is, so is he: Nabal is his name, and folly is with him! But I, your maidservant, did not see the young men of my lord whom you sent.'" 1 Samuel 25:23-25 (NKJV).

In a dramatic conclusion, Nabal's heart turns to stone upon hearing of the near disaster he had provoked, and he dies shortly after, struck down by the Lord. This narrative is rich with lessons on the nature of wisdom, the consequences of folly, and the importance of recognizing the character traits that truly matter in a partner.

The Lack of Character of Nabal

Nabal's story is a cautionary story that vividly illustrates the consequences of specific character flaws. His interactions with David reveal traits that serve as red flags in any relationship, especially a marital one. Through a closer examination of Nabal's character, we can glean essential lessons on the qualities to avoid in a potential spouse.

Lack of Respect for David, a Man of God: Nabal's response to David's polite request for provisions reveals a profound lack of respect for David and the principles of kindness and mutual support. His dismissive attitude towards David, who was already recognized as a man of God and the anointed future king of Israel, underscores Nabal's arrogance and disrespect for spiritual authority.

> "Then Nabal answered David's servants, and said, 'Who is David, and who is the son of Jesse? There are many servants nowadays who break away each one from his master. Shall I then take my bread and my water and my meat that I have killed for my shearers, and give it to men when I do not know where they are from?'" 1 Samuel 25:10-11 (NKJV).

Wrong Judgment and Prejudice Against David: Nabal's refusal to help David was not just a denial of assistance; it was based on a prejudiced and erroneous judgment of David's character. He equated David with a rebellious servant, failing to recognize or acknowledge the good David had done for his own shepherds. This wrongful judgment of David's character and intentions highlights Nabal's predisposition to prejudice and inability to discern truth from hearsay.

Lack of Hospitality and Generosity: The virtue of hospitality, highly esteemed in biblical times as it is now, was notably absent in Nabal's character. Despite his considerable wealth and the minimal impact that assisting David would have had on his resources, Nabal chose to withhold help. This lack of generosity and hospitality, especially towards those in need, marked him as someone who lacked compassion and the willingness to support others.

Self-centeredness and Trust in His Own Wealth: Nabal's self-centered attitude is most evident in his boastful reliance on his possessions. His reaction to David's request reflects a deeper trust in his own wealth and achievements rather than in God's provision and the importance of community and relationships. This self-reliance not only isolated him from those around him but also blinded him to the needs and well-being of others.

Tendency to Pay Good with Evil: A striking aspect of Nabal's character was his inclination to repay good with evil. Despite the protection David and his men provided for Nabal's shepherds, Nabal responded with contempt and insult when approached for assistance. This response showcases a lack of gratitude and a deep-seated malice unworthy of emulation.

> *"Surely in vain I have protected all that this fellow has in the wilderness, so that nothing was missed of all that belongs to him. And he has repaid me evil for good."* 1 Samuel 25:21 (NKJV)

Self-Opinionated Nature: Nabal's interactions reveal him as exceedingly self-opinionated, to the point of being impervious to counsel or reason. This trait is highlighted by his servants, who saw him as someone impossible to reason with, epitomizing the danger of pride and arrogance clouding judgment.

> *"Now therefore, know and consider what you will do, for harm is determined against our master and against all his household. For he is such a scoundrel that one cannot speak to him."* 1 Samuel 25:17 (NKJV)

Given to Wine: Nabal's penchant for drunkenness further underscores his folly. His indulgence to the point of inebriation at a feast, oblivious to the grave danger his household was in due to his actions, exemplifies a lifestyle marred by excess and lack of self-control. The Bible warns against such behavior, cautioning that "wine is a mocker" (Proverbs 20:1), and indeed, Nabal's end was precipitated by his drunken stupor.

> *"Now Abigail went to Nabal, and there he was, holding a feast in his house, like the feast of a king. And Nabal's heart was merry within him, for he was very drunk; therefore, she told him nothing, little or much, until morning light. So it was, in the morning, when the wine had gone from Nabal, and his wife had told him these things, that his heart died within him, and he became like a stone. Then it happened, after about ten days, that the LORD struck Nabal, and he died."* 1 Samuel 25:36-38 (NKJV)

Nabal's story culminates in a divine judgment that underscores the seriousness of his folly. After Abigail's intervention prevented David from exacting vengeance, Nabal's heart turned to stone upon learning of the near catastrophe his actions had almost caused. Shortly after that, "the Lord struck Nabal, and he died" 1 Samuel 25:38 (NKJV), a fate that serves as a stark reminder of the consequences of living a life marked by folly, disrespect, and disregard for God and others.

> *"So it was, in the morning, when the wine had gone from Nabal, and his wife had told him these things, that his heart died within him, and he became like a stone. Then it happened, after about ten days, that the LORD struck Nabal, and he died."* 1 Samuel 25:37-38 (NKJV).

Nabal's life and interactions with David provide a vivid illustration of how certain negative traits can harm relationships with others and ultimately lead to one's downfall. His story serves as a cautionary example of the characteristics to be wary of in choosing a life partner, emphasizing the importance of respect, generosity, humility, and a heart aligned with God's values.

Lessons from Abigail's Response

In stark contrast to Nabal's harshness and folly stands the figure of Abigail, his wife, whose response to a potentially catastrophic situation highlights virtues of wisdom, hospitality, and decisive action. Abigail's intervention in the narrative averts a disaster and serves as a beacon of righteous behavior, offering profound lessons on how to conduct oneself in relationships and conflicts.

Abigail's Wisdom and Hospitality: Upon learning of her husband's grievous insult to David and the impending doom it invited, Abigail wasted no time crafting a response marked by intelligence and generosity. Recognizing the gravity of the situation, she quickly gathered provisions and set out to meet David, intending to make amends for her husband's actions.

> "Then Abigail made haste, and took two hundred loaves, and two bottles of wine, and five sheep ready dressed, and five measures of parched corn, and an hundred clusters of raisins, and two hundred cakes of figs, and laid them on asses." 1 Samuel 25:18 (NKJV).

Her actions demonstrate a deep understanding of hospitality as a tool for reconciliation and peacemaking. By offering sustenance to David and his men, she met their immediate physical needs and extended an olive branch that signaled respect and acknowledgment of David's rightful grievances.

Quick Action to Remedy Her Husband's Folly: Abigail's swift response underscores the importance of timely intervention in preventing the escalation of conflict. Upon meeting David, her words were filled with humility and wisdom, appealing to David's better nature and God's justice, thereby dissuading him from shedding blood in vengeance.

> *"So she fell at his feet and said: 'On me, my lord, on me let this iniquity be! And please let your maidservant speak in your ears, and hear the words of your maidservant.'"* 1 Samuel 25:24, (NKJV)

Her plea to David highlights her exceptional discernment and understanding of the broader implications of his planned retribution. Through her intervention, Abigail exemplifies the power of wise words and thoughtful actions in altering the course of events, showcasing the potential of virtue to transform situations filled with anger and potential violence into ones of forgiveness and peace.

From Abigail's intervention, we learn the importance of taking responsibility, even for situations not of our own making, and the strength of character it takes to seek reconciliation rather than conflict. Her story illuminates the biblical principle found in Proverbs 15:1, *"A gentle answer turns away wrath, but a harsh word stirs up anger,"* (NIV) demonstrating the transformative power of a gentle and wise approach in resolving disputes and fostering harmony.

Abigail's response to the crisis provoked by Nabal's folly serves as a timeless lesson in the virtues of wisdom, hospitality, and proactive peacemaking. Her actions not only averted a tragedy but also left an indelible mark on the biblical narrative, providing a model of godly behavior that starkly contrasts the destructive path of foolishness and pride.

The Dangers of Marrying a Nabal

Marrying someone who embodies Nabal's negative traits—arrogance, disrespect, lack of generosity, drunkenness, and self-centeredness—can have profound implications on one's personal well-being, spiritual growth, and relations within the community. Such traits in a partner can lead to a marriage filled with conflict, misunderstandings, and emotional pain. The lack of respect and understanding can stifle personal growth and lead to a spiritually unfulfilling life, as the relationship lacks the mutual support and encouragement needed for individuals to flourish in their faith.

Moreover, a partner with Nabal-like characteristics can strain relations with friends, family, and the broader community. Their inability to show hospitality, kindness, and generosity not only isolates the couple from potential support networks but also can tarnish their reputation and relationships within their community. The ripple effects of such behavior can lead to isolation and conflict, affecting not just the couple but also those around them.

In today's context, recognizing a "Nabal" requires discernment and an understanding of the traits that define such a character. Key indicators include a consistent pattern of disrespectful behavior, an arrogant and unyielding attitude, a lack of empathy and generosity, and a tendency to prioritize one's own needs and desires over those of others. Additionally, a disregard for spiritual values and a tendency to react negatively to advice or correction can be telltale signs.

It's crucial to look beyond superficial qualities and external attributes like wealth or social status, focusing instead on the person's character, values, and how they treat others. Seeking God's wisdom through prayer and reflection is essential in discerning these traits, as is observing how the individual behaves in various situations, particularly under stress or when they believe they are unobserved.

Practical Steps for Avoiding a Nabal

When red flags indicative of Nabal-like traits are identified, several practical steps can be taken to avoid entering into a harmful relationship:

Prayer and Divine Guidance: The first step should always be to seek God's guidance through prayer, asking for discernment and wisdom in understanding the situation and knowing how to proceed.

Consult Spiritual Leaders: Engaging with trusted spiritual leaders, mentors, or counselors can provide valuable perspective and advice. With their experience and understanding of biblical principles, these individuals can offer insights that you might overlook or be too emotionally involved to see clearly.

Heed Warning Signs: Do not ignore red flags or write them off as minor issues. It's important to take serious concerns about a potential partner's character or behavior to heart, considering their long-term implications.

Prioritize Character Over External Attributes: Remember that qualities like kindness, generosity, respect, and spiritual maturity are far more valuable in a life partner than material wealth or status. Prioritize these internal attributes in your decision-making process.

By taking these steps, individuals can better navigate the complexities of relationships, avoiding the pitfalls of being unequally yoked with someone who exhibits Nabal-like traits. The goal is to find a partner who shares your values and aspirations, enriches your life, supports your spiritual journey, and contributes positively to your relationships with others in the community.

A Warning

Should you choose to marry someone with traits akin to Nabal's, be prepared for the following realities:

Frequent Need for Damage Control: You may find yourself constantly mitigating the fallout from his unwise actions in public settings. The necessity to apologize or smooth over relations can become a regular part of your life.

Enduring the Effects of Excessive Drinking: Brace yourself for the challenges that accompany a partner given to overindulgence in alcohol. The repercussions of such a lifestyle—ranging from health issues to unpredictable behavior—will inevitably impact your life together.

A Lack of Generosity and Hospitality: Prepare to forego the joy and blessings that come from a spirit of generosity and hospitality. A partner who lacks empathy for others, especially those in need, falls short of the divine expectation to *"love your neighbor as yourself"* (Mark 12:31).

Potential Retaliation from Those Wronged: The actions of a spouse who habitually mistreats or offends others may expose you to the risk of retribution from those he has aggrieved. The community's response to his behavior could directly affect your safety and well-being.

The Prospect of Premature Widowhood: It's a sobering consideration, but aligning your life with someone who embodies Nabal's characteristics might increase the likelihood of finding yourself alone sooner than anticipated. The lifestyle and choices of a "Nabal" can lead to outcomes that prematurely end his life, leaving you to navigate the future on your own.

Final Thoughts

The cautionary tale of Nabal, as chronicled in the Scriptures, is a powerful reminder of the profound impact that character traits can have on relationships, especially within the sanctity of marriage. Nabal's story, juxtaposed with the wisdom and grace of Abigail, offers us invaluable insights into the importance of discernment, the virtues of kindness and generosity, and the dangers of pride and folly.

As we reflect on the narrative and its implications for choosing a life partner, it becomes evident that the decision to marry should not be taken lightly. It demands a deep evaluation of character beyond surface-level attractions or material considerations. The traits embodied by Nabal — disrespect, arrogance, lack of hospitality, and self-indulgence — serve as red flags that cannot be ignored if one seeks a marriage grounded in mutual respect, love, and spiritual growth.

In navigating the path toward marriage, let us be guided by the wisdom of Scripture and the example of those who have walked in faith before us. Let us seek partners who embody the virtues of kindness, humility, generosity, and a deep love for God and His people. These are the qualities that build a foundation for a strong, enduring, and godly marriage.

Furthermore, let us approach this significant life decision with prayer, seeking God's guidance and wisdom above all. The journey of marriage is one of partnership, where two individuals come together to support, cherish, and uplift one another in all aspects of life. Choosing a spouse, therefore, is not merely about finding someone with whom to share our lives but about finding a companion who will walk with us on the path of faith, growing together toward the likeness of Christ.

Chapter 3

Don't Rush to Marry an Amnon

Marriage: If you want something to last forever, you treat it differently. You shield it and protect it. You never abuse it. You don't expose it to the elements. You don't make it common or ordinary. If it ever becomes tarnished, you lovingly polish it until it gleams like new. It becomes special because you have made it so, and it grows more beautiful and precious as time goes by.

— F. Burton Howard

In the quest for a life partner, the allure of immediate attraction or superficial qualities can often overshadow the crucial evaluation of character and intentions. The biblical account of Amnon and Tamar stands as a stark reminder of the devastating consequences that can arise from lust, deceit, and unchecked desires. This narrative reveals the dark side of human nature and serves as a cautionary tale about the importance of recognizing unhealthy behaviors in potential partners. By examining Amnon's actions and their aftermath, we can glean vital insights into the red flags that must not be ignored in any relationship.

The unsettling story of Amnon and Tamar is recounted in 2 Samuel 13, providing a detailed look into the dangers of unbridled lust and manipulation. Amnon, one of King David's sons, became infatuated with his half-sister Tamar, a virgin renowned for her beauty. His obsession with Tamar was so intense that he fell into a state of melancholy, pondering over a way to fulfill his desires, as it was improper for him to have any romantic involvement with her due to their familial relationship.

> "After this Absalom the son of David had a lovely sister, whose name was Tamar; and Amnon the son of David loved her. Amnon was so distressed over his sister Tamar that he became sick; for she was a virgin. And it was improper for Amnon to do anything to her." 2 Samuel 13:1-2, (NKJV)

zIn desperation, Amnon resorted to deceit, influenced by the cunning advice of Jonadab, a friend and cousin. Jonadab proposed a ruse: Amnon was to feign illness and request that Tamar be sent to prepare food for him, allowing him to be alone with her.

> "So Jonadab said to him, 'Lie down on your bed and pretend to be ill. And when your father comes to see you, say to him, 'Please let my sister Tamar come and give me food, and prepare the food in my sight, that I may see it and eat it from her hand.'" 2 Samuel 13:5 (NKJV)

Unaware of Amnon's true intentions, King David sent Tamar to care for her brother. Seizing the opportunity, Amnon carried out his vile plan, forcefully raping Tamar despite her pleas for reason. Following the act, Amnon's "love" turned into intense hatred, and he callously rejected Tamar, exacerbating her desolation and shame.

> *"Then Amnon hated her exceedingly, so that the hatred with which he hated her was greater than the love with which he had loved her. And Amnon said to her, 'Arise, be gone!'"* 2 Samuel 13:15, (NKJV)

The aftermath of this heinous act reverberated through David's household, culminating in Absalom's revenge and Amnon's death two years later, illustrating the far-reaching consequences of Amnon's lust and deception.

This narrative starkly illustrates Amnon's reprehensible character and actions, serving as a biblical example of the perils of allowing lustful desires and deceit to dictate one's actions. The story of Amnon and Tamar warns of the importance of discerning underlying motives and behaviors in relationships, emphasizing the need for vigilance in recognizing warning signs that could lead to harm.

Amnon's Lack of Character

Amnon's willingness to manipulate and deceive to satisfy this desire reflects a character deeply marred by selfishness and a lack of moral grounding. The role of deceit in Amnon's strategy is particularly telling. Advised by Jonadab, Amnon crafts a scheme that exploits the trust and concern of both his father, King David, and Tamar. This manipulation underscores a disturbing willingness to use deceit as a tool for personal gain, revealing a character that values the fulfillment of lustful intentions over honesty and integrity. Such behavior not only leads to his moral degradation but also sets the stage for the tragic violation of Tamar.

Moreover, Amnon's lack of self-control is evident in his inability to restrain his desires or consider the consequences of his actions. This deficit, coupled with his abrupt shift from an obsessive desire to intense hatred towards Tamar post-act, illustrates the volatile and transient nature of lust that is not grounded in genuine affection or respect. The immediate reversal of his feelings towards Tamar after he had violated her speaks to a profound inner emptiness and a lack of genuine emotional connection, highlighting the destructive nature of lust when divorced from love and responsibility.

The Dangers of Lust and Deceit in Relationships

Lust, especially when it seeks fulfillment at the expense of another's well-being, erodes the dignity and respect crucial to any relationship. It prioritizes temporary gratification over lasting connection, inevitably leading to harm and disillusionment.

Deceit, as employed by Amnon, further undermines the trust essential to any meaningful relationship's fabric. Trust, once broken, is challenging to rebuild, and relationships marred by deceit often struggle to recover. The use of manipulation and lies to achieve selfish ends reveals a lack of character and integrity, traits that are fundamental to a healthy partnership.

The combination of lust and deceit creates a toxic environment that stifles growth, mutual respect, and genuine intimacy. Relationships founded on such shaky ground will likely be characterized by instability, unhappiness, and conflict. The story of Amnon and Tamar starkly illustrates how allowing lustful desires and deceitful tactics to dictate one's actions can lead to personal ruin and cause profound harm to others.

In navigating relationships, it is crucial to cultivate qualities such as honesty, self-control, respect, and genuine affection. These values foster trust, deepen emotional connection, and build a robust and healthy foundation that can withstand the challenges of life. By reflecting on the lessons from Amnon's story, individuals can strive to avoid the pitfalls of lust and deceit, instead choosing paths that lead to fulfilling and respectful relationships.

Identifying Traits of Modern-Day Amnons

In the quest for genuine connections, it's crucial to be vigilant of individuals who embody the characteristics of Amnon, often hidden beneath a veneer of charm and intense attraction. These modern Amnons, driven by their desires, may resort to manipulation, creating elaborate facades to ensnare others emotionally. Their deceitful tactics, mirroring Amnon's pretense of illness, are designed to exploit empathy and lower defenses, all in the pursuit of personal gratification.

The hallmark of Amnon's approach is the suspension of shame. Pushing boundaries under the guise of love, they advocate for intimacy devoid of marital commitment, blatantly disregarding the values and comfort of others. This brazenness is often justified with hollow promises or distorted interpretations of love, seeking to erode the resolve of those they pursue.

After the pursuit, as with Amnon, there's often a stark shift in demeanor—from fervent desire to indifference or even disdain. This sudden change reveals a profound lack of genuine emotional attachment, highlighting a relationship based on convenience rather than deep affection.

Moreover, the Amnons of today are characterized by an unrelenting pursuit of sexual satisfaction. This relentless demand often places undue strain on relationships, leading to emotional weariness and, in some cases, the betrayal of trust through infidelity. Their early and pressing demands for physical intimacy serve as a litmus test for their affections, falsely equating love with sexual compliance.

Strategies for Recognition and Protection

Recognizing the warning signs of an Amnon requires a discerning eye and an unwavering commitment to godly values and emotional well-being. Key indicators include a rapid escalation of affection, manipulation or deceit in interactions, a disregard for mutual consent, and volatile shifts in attention or affection.

Maintaining a critical perspective on the intentions behind grand gestures or promises can safeguard against manipulation. Consulting with trusted friends or pastors about concerns can provide clarity and reassurance, offering a balanced perspective on the relationship.

Establishing and asserting personal boundaries early on is paramount. A genuine partner respects these limits and values your comfort and consent above their desires. Observing how they react to boundaries can be telling of their true nature.

Lastly, embracing patience and wisdom in developing a relationship allows for the gradual building of trust and understanding, laying the foundation for a connection that transcends mere physical attraction or fleeting desires.

Consequences of Overlooking Red Flags

Ignoring red flags in a partner's behavior, especially those that mirror Amnon's traits, can lead to a spectrum of adverse outcomes. The story of Amnon and Tamar is not just a cautionary tale of ancient times; it reflects real and present dangers in overlooking warning signs in relationships. The consequences of such oversight can be profound, affecting one's emotional well-being, spiritual health, and relational dynamics.

Emotional Consequences: Being in a relationship with someone who prioritizes lustful desires over respect and consent can lead to deep emotional scars. Victims may suffer from a range of issues, including anxiety, depression, and low self-esteem. The betrayal of trust and the violation of personal boundaries can leave lasting wounds, impacting one's ability to form healthy relationships in the future. The emotional turmoil of feeling used and discarded, as Tamar must have felt, can also lead to isolation and a profound sense of worthlessness.

Spiritual Consequences: Spiritually, being entangled with a partner who exhibits Amnon-like behavior can lead to a disconnection from one's faith and values. The guilt, shame, and confusion that arise from being in such a relationship can make it challenging to engage with one's church or to seek solace in spiritual practices. The inner conflict between one's beliefs and the reality of the relationship can erode one's faith foundation, leading to a spiritual crisis.

Relational Consequences: On a relational level, overlooking red flags can result in a toxic and abusive dynamic that undermines the very foundation of trust and mutual respect essential for a healthy relationship. This dynamic can extend beyond the couple, affecting family and friends who may feel powerless to help or become estranged in the process. Furthermore, the example set by such a relationship can have ripple effects, influencing how others perceive and engage in their own relationships.

Real-Life Implications: In real life, being with someone who values gratification over genuine connection can mean enduring a cycle of emotional highs and lows, with the inherent instability leaving one constantly on edge. The lack of true intimacy and understanding can result in a lonely and unfulfilling partnership, where one's needs and feelings are consistently disregarded. For those who dream of a future built on mutual love, respect, and shared values, ignoring warning signs can derail those aspirations, leading to a reality marked by conflict, dissatisfaction, and regret.

The consequences of overlooking red flags in a partner's behavior are far-reaching, impacting one's emotional health, spiritual well-being, and the quality of both current and future relationships. Recognizing and addressing these warning signs early can prevent significant harm and lead to healthier, more fulfilling relationships that align with one's values and aspirations. As we navigate the complexities of relationships, let us be guided by wisdom, discernment, and a commitment to our own well-being and that of our loved ones.

Practical Steps for Avoidance and Healing

In navigating the complexities of relationships, particularly those that may bear the warning signs of harmful behavior reminiscent of Amnon, practical steps can be taken to protect oneself and foster healing from past hurts. Here are some strategies to consider:

Prioritize Prayer and Divine Guidance: Making prayer a foundational aspect of your relationship decisions invites divine wisdom into the process. Seek God's guidance with an open heart, asking for discernment to recognize traits and behaviors that may be harmful. Prayer can also bring peace and clarity, especially when feelings and attractions might cloud judgment.

Consult Spiritual Leaders: Engaging in conversations with spiritual mentors, pastors, or trusted church leaders who have your best interests at heart can provide valuable outside perspectives. These individuals can offer counsel based on their experiences, wisdom, and understanding of what constitutes a healthy, godly relationship.

Establish and Maintain Healthy Boundaries: Setting clear personal boundaries is essential for any healthy relationship. These boundaries should respect your values, emotional well-being, and physical safety. Be upfront about your expectations and limits and observe whether they are respected. Boundaries not only protect you but also serve as a test of character for the other person.

Practice Self-Respect: Honoring yourself, your values, and your worth is crucial. Remember that you deserve to be treated with respect, kindness, and dignity. A partner who truly values you will honor your boundaries, support your dreams, and contribute positively to your growth and well-being.

Final Takeaway

The biblical account of Amnon and Tamar provides powerful lessons on the dangers of lust, deceit, and disregarding the well-being of others. It underscores the importance of vigilance in recognizing unhealthy traits in potential partners and reminds us of the profound impact our relationship choices can have on our lives.

As we reflect on Amnon's story, let us reaffirm the value of patience, wisdom, and discernment in pursuing a life partner. True love and compatibility are built on a foundation of mutual respect, shared values, and genuine affection, not fleeting desires or manipulative behaviors.

May we approach our relationships guided by prayer, seeking God's wisdom and guidance in every step. For those healing from past hurts, may you find strength and renewal in God's unwavering love and grace. And for those seeking a partner, may you be blessed with the discernment to recognize the qualities that lead to a healthy, fulfilling relationship.

Let us close this chapter with a prayer:

Heavenly Father, grant us the wisdom to discern the intentions of those we allow into our lives. Help us recognize warning signs and seek relationships that honor You. Provide strength and healing to those wounded by past relationships and guide us all in making choices that lead to love, joy, and peace. In Jesus' name, we pray, Amen.

Through the lessons learned from Amnon's story, may we all move forward with a deeper understanding of what it means to choose well, love wisely, and live in accordance with God's design for relationships.

Chapter 4

Don't Rush To Marry An Ahab

In a godly marriage, both partners commit to dealing with their own sin, which leads to the deepening of their friendship.

— Timothy Keller

In biblical history, King Ahab stands as a figure shadowed by his own choices and the company he kept, particularly in his marriage. Scripture succinctly captures the essence of Ahab's character and reign in 1 Kings 16:30-31, stating, *"And Ahab the son of Omri did evil in the sight of the Lord more than all who were before him."* (KJV)

This statement sets the stage for a king whose reign was marked not just by personal failings but also by the profound influence of his wife. Ahab's union with Jezebel, the daughter of Ethbaal, king of the Sidonians, catalyzed a dramatic shift in Israel's spiritual landscape.

This marriage was not merely a political alliance; it was a

turning point that plunged Ahab deeper into idolatry, leading him to serve and worship Baal. The significance of this marriage cannot be overstated, as it intertwined Ahab's destiny with the propagation of idol worship, challenging the very foundation of Israel's covenant with Jehovah.

The Background Story

King Ahab's story is a vivid web of ambition, spiritual apostasy, and the consequences of turning away from God. From the onset, Ahab's actions were a departure from the ways of the Lord, plunging his reign into notoriety as he committed evils unprecedented among the kings of Israel. The scripture provides a detailed narrative of Ahab's misdeeds, each act adding to his legacy of defiance against God.

A pivotal moment in Ahab's life and reign was his marriage to Jezebel. This union was more than a mere merger of two powerful families; it was a confluence of cultures and deities that steered Ahab further away from God. Coming from a background steeped in the worship of Baal, Jezebel brought her religious practices into Israel, influencing Ahab to erect an altar for Baal in the heart of Israel, Samaria.

This act of building a house for Baal, as detailed in 1 Kings 16:31-32, was not just an addition to the landscape of Samaria; it symbolized a profound spiritual shift within Ahab and the kingdom. Ahab's willingness to embrace and promote the worship of Baal under Jezebel's influence marked a significant departure from the monotheistic worship of Jehovah, setting the stage for conflict and tragedy within the narrative of Israel's kings.

Ahab's deeds, as recounted in scripture, paint a portrait of a king ensnared by his desires and the influence of those around him. His story is a cautionary tale about the dangers of forsaking God's commandments in pursuit of personal gain and the profound impact one's choice of partner can have on one's spiritual journey and leadership. Ahab's marriage to Jezebel was not just a personal failure but a catalyst that propelled him into actions that had lasting repercussions for the kingdom of Israel, underscoring the intricate link between individual choices and public consequences.

Unbelief and Spiritual Waywardness

At the core of Ahab's failings was a profound spiritual waywardness. The king's deliberate shift from worshipping Jehovah to embracing the cult of Baal signifies more than just a change in religious observance; it represents a fundamental departure from the covenantal faith of Israel. Ahab's transition to Baal worship was not merely a passive acquiescence but an active endorsement of idolatry, underscored by his marriage to Jezebel and the subsequent construction of an altar for Baal in Samaria.

This spiritual apostasy highlights the dangers inherent in compromising one's faith, showing how easily the allure of foreign beliefs and practices can lead one astray, especially when such beliefs are introduced and supported by influential figures like Jezebel. Ahab's example serves as a cautionary reminder of the importance of steadfastness in one's spiritual convictions and the peril of allowing external influences to dictate one's relationship with the divine.

Covetousness

Another defining characteristic of Ahab's reign was his covetous nature, best exemplified by the episode involving Naboth's vineyard. Ahab's desire for Naboth's property, driven by convenience and greed, demonstrates a blatant disregard for divine law and the rights of others.

Despite Naboth's lawful refusal, based on the Lord's commandments against selling familial inheritance, Ahab's reaction—sullenness and vexation—reveals a childlike petulance and an inability to accept denial. This incident showcases Ahab's covetousness and his lack of moral fortitude, choosing personal desire over adherence to God's statutes.

The tragic outcome of Naboth's refusal, culminating in Jezebel's orchestration of his murder, further illustrates the destructive consequences of unchecked greed and the lengths to which Ahab and Jezebel were willing to go to satisfy their desires.

Weakness and Manipulability

Ahab's weakness and susceptibility to manipulation are most poignantly demonstrated in his interactions with Jezebel and her influence over his decisions. Ahab's acquiescence to Jezebel's schemes, from the establishment of Baal worship in Israel to the orchestration of Naboth's murder, underscores a profound lack of personal conviction and strength.

His failure to uphold the commandments of the Lord, swayed by Jezebel's ambitions and idolatrous practices, marks him as a king easily manipulated and led away from the path of righteousness. This weakness not only compromised his reign but also facilitated the spread of idolatry and injustice within Israel, highlighting the dangers of allowing oneself to be influenced by those who do not share a commitment to divine principles and moral integrity.

Identifying Modern-Day Ahabs

The characteristics of King Ahab, as delineated in the scriptures, find a modern parallel in individuals whose lives and relationships are significantly influenced, if not controlled, by external familial forces, particularly maternal ones. These modern Ahabs navigate their relationships under the significant sway of their mothers' opinions and desires, often at the cost of their own autonomy and the health of their romantic partnerships.

Maternal Direction Over Personal Life. Imagine a scenario where every decision, from a wedding venue to the number of children a couple plans to have, requires maternal approval. Such an 'Ahab's life' direction is not determined by personal conviction or mutual discussion with his partner but by his mother's wishes and preferences. This dynamic is akin to a remote control where the mother's input dictates the course of her son's life, relegating his partner to a secondary role.

Jonathan and Esther's wedding planning saga exemplifies this, with Jonathan's mother, Margaret, overriding their preferences for a church venue with her insistence on a traditional setting. This pattern of maternal interference makes Esther's input feel secondary, overshadowing her role in her own marriage.

Inability to Assert Independence. Consider the case of a man unable to voice his own desires if they conflict with his mother's. This Ahab-like figure exhibits a profound people-pleasing tendency, prioritizing his mother's satisfaction over his own and, by extension, over that of his partner. His fear of upsetting his mother trumps all, leading to a relationship dynamic where the partner feels perpetually sidelined.

Steven's story illustrates this point vividly, where he finds himself in a tight spot when his mother disapproves of the modern decor he and Stephanie chose for their home. Despite loving the chosen style, Steven feels compelled to return everything and select traditional pieces his mother prefers. Stephanie's frustration grows as she watches Steven struggle to assert his preferences, feeling that their home no longer represents their shared tastes but caters solely to his mother's.

Constant Need for Maternal Approval. In some relationships, the man's need for maternal approval is a silent yet powerful force. He secretly seeks to make decisions that would win his mother's nod of approval, placing her happiness above that of the relationship. This underlying allegiance can strain the partnership, especially when significant decisions are influenced more by the desire to please the mother than by the couple's mutual best interests.

For example, Daniel secretly dreams of starting a restaurant with his fiancée, Lisa. However, his mother believes he should continue his career in law. Torn between his passion and the need for his mother's approval, Daniel hesitates to pursue the venture he and Lisa are excited about. This hesitation strains their relationship as Lisa feels their dreams are being sidelined to win approval from Daniel's mother.

Perpetual Communication with Mother. The modern Ahab is in constant touch with his mother, sharing details of his life and, often, of his relationship. While seemingly innocuous, this open line of communication can infringe upon the privacy and autonomy of the romantic relationship, creating a triangulation where the mother's presence looms large over every aspect of the couple's life.

For instance, Peter and Eve notice their private discussions about starting a family somehow reach Peter's mother before they've made any decisions. During their daily calls, Peter habitually shares details of their life with his mother. Eve feels like there's a third person in their marriage, making it difficult for her to speak openly with Peter, knowing their conversations are not just between them.

Financial Dependence and Decision-Making. Financial dependence on a mother in adulthood is a red flag indicative of an Ahab-like character. When major life decisions, from housing to investments, are contingent upon maternal approval or financial contribution, it underscores a lack of independence that can erode the foundations of a marital relationship.

Nathanael and Delilah's house-hunting challenges, dictated by Nathanael's financially supportive mother, highlight the constraints of such dependence. Nathanael's inability to make autonomous choices leaves Delilah apprehensive about their future, fearing that their life together will always be under the shadow of his mother's influence.

Navigating the Challenge of Modern-Day Ahabs

Recognizing these traits is the first step in navigating relationships with potential Ahabs. Individuals must assess the dynamics of their partner's family relationships early on, seeking signs of undue influence or control. Setting healthy boundaries, fostering open communication, and ensuring mutual respect for autonomy and decision-making are essential strategies for mitigating the challenges posed by modern-day Ahabs

Ultimately, relationships thrive on equality, mutual respect, and the ability to make decisions as a couple, free from external control. Understanding and addressing the influences that mirror Ahab's traits can help couples build stronger, more independent relationships that stand on their own merits rather than on the approval or direction of others.

Marriage to a Modern-Day Ahab

Marrying a modern-day Ahab can set the stage for a challenging and frustrating marital dynamic. When translated into a contemporary marriage, the influence of Ahab's character traits predicts a series of potential issues that can profoundly affect the relationship's foundation and the personal growth of both partners.

Lack of Independent Thought. In a marriage with a modern-day Ahab, you might find that your husband's opinions and decisions are not his own but reflections or extensions of his mother's thoughts and preferences. This lack of independent thinking can make it difficult for you to connect with your husband on a genuine level. Ideally, a partnership benefits from each individual's unique perspectives, but with an Ahab, the marital dialogue may feel like a triangulation, with the mother's voice echoing your husband's words.

Overbearing Maternal Influence. The metaphorical "remote control" held by your husband's mother can turn your marriage into a constant battleground of wills, where even the most mundane decisions are subject to external scrutiny and approval. This pervasive influence can extend to the most intimate aspects of your relationship, leaving little room for autonomy or mutual decision-making. Conflicts that should be resolved within the sanctity of your partnership instead become opportunities for further maternal intervention, undermining the unity and privacy that marriage demands.

Eroded Privacy. The constant sharing of marital details with his mother creates an environment where privacy is virtually non-existent. This open-book policy means that your personal discussions, disagreements, and plans are relayed to an external party, often without your consent. The sanctity of marital confidentiality is breached, eroding trust and intimacy between you and your husband, as the foundational principle that what happens within a marriage should remain within the marriage is disregarded.

Absence of Traditional Husbandly Qualities. An Ahab's upbringing under a dominant maternal figure can result in a lack of understanding of how to embody the role of a husband in its full capacity. The qualities contributing to a balanced and supportive partnership may be underdeveloped or absent, not due to a lack of willingness but a lack of modeled behavior and independence in his formative years. This can leave a void in the relationship, where you might find yourself compensating for his inability to assert himself in situations that require leadership, support, or protection.

Strategies for Navigating Relationships with Potential Ahabs

Engaging in a relationship with someone who exhibits traits reminiscent of Ahab can be challenging, but it's possible to navigate these waters more smoothly with the right strategies. Setting clear boundaries is crucial; this involves defining what is acceptable and what isn't within the relationship, particularly concerning the influence of external opinions. Communication about these boundaries must be open, honest, and respectful, ensuring both partners understand and agree.

Seeking spiritual discernment offers another layer of guidance, helping to distinguish between genuine affection and potentially manipulative behaviors. This can be achieved through prayer, meditation, and counsel from trusted church leaders. These practices can provide clarity and insight, aiding in making informed decisions about the relationship.

Mutual respect and independence are the bedrock of any healthy relationship. Each partner should feel free to express their thoughts, beliefs, and desires without fear of judgment or undue influence. Encouraging personal autonomy allows each individual to grow and contribute to the relationship from a place of strength and wholeness.

The story of Ahab, while ancient, provides timeless insights into the impact of external influences on personal and relational integrity. Modern relationships can suffer when one partner lacks the autonomy or spiritual integrity to stand firm in their convictions, mirroring the challenges seen in Ahab's life.

As we reflect on these lessons, it becomes clear that the foundation of a strong relationship lies in choosing a partner who values spiritual integrity, personal autonomy, and mutual respect. These qualities enable couples to face life's challenges together, making decisions that honor both their individual and shared values.

Chapter 5

Don't Rush to Marry a Solomon

A good marriage isn't something you find; it's something you make, and you have to keep on making it.

— Gary Thomas

In the annals of biblical history, King Solomon emerges as a figure of profound complexity, embodying a paradox that resonates through the ages. Chosen by God to succeed his father, David, Solomon is celebrated for his divine appointment and unparalleled wisdom and wealth. His reign, marked by peace and prosperity, symbolizes the pinnacle of Israel's glory in the ancient world. Yet, beneath the surface of these remarkable achievements lies a narrative of personal choices and relational dynamics fraught with cautionary tales.

Solomon's story is emblematic of the human condition, illustrating how the very wisdom that sets one apart can also lead to one's downfall when not anchored in obedience to God. This chapter seeks to unravel the enigma of Solomon, drawing attention to the lessons embedded in his life's story, primarily concerning marital relationships. It is a tale that warns against the allure of external achievements and calls for a deeper examination of the spiritual and moral fiber that should guide our connections with others.

Solomon's Wisdom and Wealth

The biblical account of Solomon's ascension to the throne is a testament to his unique relationship with God. In a dream at Gibeon, God offered Solomon anything he desired. Eschewing wealth, long life, or the death of his enemies, Solomon chose wisdom — an understanding heart to judge God's people and discern between good and evil (1 Kings 3:5-14). This request pleased the Lord, who not only granted him unparalleled wisdom but also bestowed upon him riches and honor beyond any king before or after him.

1 Kings 4:29-34 paints a vivid portrait of Solomon's wisdom and its manifestations. *"God gave Solomon wisdom and exceedingly great understanding, and largeness of heart like the sand on the seashore."* (NKJV) His wisdom surpassed all the wisdom of the East and Egypt, making him wiser than any other man. Solomon's repertoire of knowledge was vast, spanning proverbs, songs, and discourses on the natural world — from the cedar of Lebanon to the hyssop that springs from the wall and from animals and birds to reptiles and fish. Such was the breadth and depth of his understanding that kings from every nation and men from all walks of life came to listen to the wisdom Solomon had been endowed with by God.

This narrative sets the stage for a reign that would be remembered as much for its intellectual and material prosperity as for the spiritual and moral dilemmas it would engender. Solomon's wisdom, a divine gift meant to build and govern a people according to God's will, would paradoxically lead him down paths that diverged from the very principles he was chosen to uphold. As we delve deeper into Solomon's story, it becomes evident that his relational decisions, especially his marriages, would have profound implications not just for his personal spirituality but for the entire nation of Israel.

In exploring Solomon's wisdom and wealth, we are reminded of the dual nature of such gifts — they can lead to outstanding achievements and acclaim. Still, they can also become stumbling blocks when not tempered by fidelity to God's commandments. Solomon's life invites us to reflect on the true source of wisdom and the importance of aligning our gifts and blessings with God's purposes, especially in the area of relationships.

The Caution Against Marrying a Solomon

While Solomon's wisdom and wealth are lauded throughout biblical history, his story serves as a nuanced cautionary tale, particularly in the context of relationships. The distinction lies not in the wisdom itself, a divine gift Solomon used to lead Israel to unprecedented heights, but in how he allowed his other, less admirable traits to overshadow this wisdom.

Solomon, for all his understanding, faltered by placing his personal desires and achievements above the commandments of God. This crucial aspect of Solomon's character warrants careful consideration for anyone seeking a partner. Admiring someone for their intellect, talents, or material success is natural, but it's imperative to discern whether these attributes are coupled with spiritual integrity and obedience to divine principles.

Solomon's disregard for God's commandments, especially concerning marriage, highlights the dangers of being entwined with someone who prioritizes their desires over spiritual laws. Despite the explicit prohibitions against marrying outside of the faith to prevent idolatry (Deuteronomy 7:3-4), Solomon's alliances with foreign women led him down a path of spiritual compromise. His marriages were not just personal failings but had national repercussions, introducing idol worship into Israel and leading the king himself away from God.

Solomon's Disregard for Divine Commandments

Solomon's marital choices starkly illustrate his departure from God's commands. His union with numerous foreign women directly contravened God's explicit instructions to Israel to avoid intermarriages with non-believers. This wasn't merely a prohibition against cultural or social mixing but a safeguard against the dilution of Israel's faith and worship practices. Solomon's defiance of this commandment didn't merely reflect personal weakness; it represented a fundamental misalignment with the covenant relationship between God and Israel.

The consequences of Solomon's choices were profound. The king who had built the Temple, establishing a fixed place for God's presence among His people, ultimately led Israel into idolatry. 1 Kings 11:1-6 details Solomon's descent into apostasy, as his heart turned after other gods, influenced by his foreign wives. This narrative isn't just a historical recounting of one king's failings but a vivid illustration of the spiritual peril inherent in aligning oneself with a partner who disregards God's laws. Solomon's wisdom could not shield him from the spiritual declension that resulted from his disobedience.

Examples Illustrating Modern-Day Solomons

Consider Michael, a man of notable intellect and charm, who has climbed the ladder of success in his career. His achievements are many, and his social media profiles are testaments to a life filled with accolades. Yet, beneath the surface of this glittering exterior, Michael's spiritual life is barren.

In relationships, he places his ambitions and ego at the forefront, often neglecting the spiritual and emotional needs of his partner, Sarah. Sarah admires Michael's brilliance and the life of comfort he provides. Still, she yearns for a deeper spiritual connection, one that Michael dismisses as unnecessary, prioritizing his career and social status over the cultivation of their spiritual journey together.

Then there's Ethan, who, like Solomon, has a wide range of interests and is open to exploring various spiritual practices. When he meets Leah, who holds her faith as a central pillar of her life, there's an initial agreement to respect each other's beliefs.

However, as their relationship progresses, Ethan begins introducing practices and ideologies that starkly contrast with Leah's faith, pressuring her to accept these as part of their life together. Leah finds herself torn between her love for Ethan and her commitment to her Christian values, mirroring the internal conflict faced by Israel under Solomon's rule as foreign gods were introduced into the heart of their worship.

Solomon's Ultimate Downfall

Solomon's story reaches a somber conclusion, marked by a departure from the very wisdom that defined his reign. His indulgence in relationships with foreign women, contrary to God's commandments, was not merely a personal failing but a pivot point that led to widespread idolatry across Israel. Solomon's temples to foreign gods stood as symbols of his spiritual adultery, a betrayal that estranged him from the Lord, who had appeared to him twice, blessing him with wisdom and wealth beyond compare.

The repercussions of Solomon's actions extended beyond his personal spirituality, casting a long shadow over the kingdom of Israel. The unity and prosperity experienced under his rule began to fracture, setting the stage for the eventual division of the kingdom. His legacy, once defined by wisdom and splendor, was tarnished by the consequences of his choices, serving as a potent reminder of the destructive potential of turning away from God's path.

Solomon's downfall underscores a profound truth: intellectual achievements, wealth, and charisma can never substitute for spiritual integrity and obedience to God. His story is a warning for the modern day, highlighting the importance of aligning one's life, including relationships, with God's commandments and spiritual truths. For those navigating the complexities of love and partnership, Solomon's narrative offers a timeless lesson on the necessity of choosing a path that honors God above all, ensuring that the foundation of any relationship is built on shared spiritual values and commitment to walking in obedience to God's will.

Identifying Modern-Day Solomons

In today's context, Solomon-like figures may not rule kingdoms or speak in proverbs. However, their characteristics can still profoundly impact relationships, particularly when their personal desires or disobedience to spiritual principles overshadow shared values and beliefs. Recognizing these modern-day Solomons requires vigilance to certain behaviors and attitudes that mirror Solomon's less admirable traits.

Excessive Emphasis on Material Success: Individuals who measure life's value solely by achievements, wealth, and status might neglect the spiritual and emotional depth of a relationship. Like Solomon, who accumulated wealth and accolades, they might focus more on external success than nurturing a shared spiritual journey with their partner.

Disregard for Spiritual Commitments: Solomon's drift from God's commandments is a warning sign for those whose partners show little regard for spiritual practices or commitments. When someone consistently chooses personal desires or societal trends over the principles that form the foundation of their shared beliefs, it may indicate a path diverging from spiritual unity.

Prioritizing Personal Desires Over Collective Well-being: Just as Solomon's indulgence led him away from

God, individuals who consistently place their wants and needs above the relationship's collective well-being may risk maintaining a balanced and spiritually aligned partnership. This self-centered approach can erode the mutual support and understanding crucial for a thriving relationship.

Red Flags

Neglect of Spiritual Growth: A partner who shows little interest in the things of God or spiritual growth, dismissing them as unimportant or irrelevant, might not support or engage in the shared spiritual journey that strengthens a relationship.

Inflexibility on Integrating Beliefs in God: If discussions about integrating beliefs in God into the relationship are met with resistance or indifference, it could signal a deeper misalignment with the spiritual foundation crucial for long-term unity.

Rationalization of Contrary Behaviors: Justifying actions or beliefs that clearly contradict the agreed-upon godly values of the relationship, much like Solomon's rationalization of his marriages and idol worship, is a red flag that personal desires are prioritized over collective spiritual health.

Visible Discomfort with Spiritual Discussions: An unmistakable sign of a modern-day Solomon can be their discomfort or outright avoidance of conversations about faith, spiritual responsibilities, and how these should influence your life together.

Identifying these traits and red flags in a potential partner is not about judgment but discernment. It involves recognizing when someone's actions and priorities might lead you away from the shared spiritual path you envision for your relationship. Engaging in open, honest discussions about spiritual beliefs, expectations, and commitments from the outset can help discern whether a potential partner will support or hinder your mutual spiritual journey.

Strategies for Navigating Relationships with Potential Solomons

Navigating a relationship with someone who exhibits Solomon-like traits requires careful consideration and proactive strategies to ensure that both partners can grow together spiritually and maintain a relationship that honors God.

Seek Partners with Spiritual Integrity: Prioritize finding a partner who values spiritual integrity and possesses wisdom that aligns with divine principles. Look for someone who demonstrates a commitment to living out their faith and places God at the center of their life. This foundational compatibility is crucial for building a relationship that can withstand challenges and grow deeper with time.

Open Communication about Spiritual Beliefs: Establish open lines of communication regarding spiritual beliefs and practices from the beginning. Discuss how your faith influences your decisions, expectations, and life goals. This transparency fosters mutual understanding and respect for each other's spiritual journey and helps identify areas where you can grow together.

Mutual Respect for Shared Convictions: Respect for each other's convictions is paramount. Even when disagreements arise, approach them with empathy and a willingness to understand your partner's perspective. Mutual respect builds a strong foundation for a relationship where both partners feel valued and heard.

Willingness to Grow Together in Faith: Commit to growing together in your spiritual journeys. This could mean participating in church activities, studying scripture together, or engaging in united prayer. Growth in faith as a couple strengthens your bond and ensures that your relationship reflects the values you both cherish.

Solomon's narrative offers timeless insights into the importance of choosing a life partner who shares your spiritual values and commitment to God. While Solomon's wisdom and wealth are admirable, his story reminds us of the pitfalls of deviating from God's commandments in pursuit of personal desires. In the modern context, this translates into the importance of seeking a partner who prioritizes spiritual integrity and mutual growth in faith.

Red Flags for Men

Chapter 6

Don't Rush To Marry A Jezebel

Let your fountain be blessed, and rejoice in the wife of your youth, a lovely deer, a graceful doe."

— Proverbs 5:18, (ESV)

Few figures in biblical history are as enigmatic and controversial as Jezebel. Born into royalty, she was the daughter of Ethbaal, King of Sidon, an area steeped in the worship of pagan gods, with Baal at the pinnacle of their pantheon. Her marriage to Ahab, the son of Omri and king of Israel, marked a pivotal moment not only in her life but in the spiritual trajectory of Israel itself. This union, detailed in 1 Kings 16:31, was not merely a political alliance but a catalyst for one of the most tumultuous periods in Israel's history.

Jezebel's arrival in Israel was the harbinger of profound religious and moral upheaval. With her, she brought the worship of

Baal and Asherah, integrating these into the fabric of Israelite society and challenging the monotheistic worship of Yahweh. Her influence over Ahab was undeniable; under her sway, Ahab constructed an altar for Baal in the heart of Samaria and erected an Asherah pole, acts that were seen as direct affronts to God and a departure from the faith of their ancestors.

But Jezebel's impact was not limited to religious reformations. She wielded her power with a ruthlessness that had seldom been seen. The prophets of the Lord were slaughtered at her command, as recounted in 1 Kings 18:4, in her quest to eradicate the worship of Yahweh from Israel. Her actions against Naboth, a man who merely wished to keep his ancestral vineyard, underscore the depths of her wickedness. By orchestrating false charges and ensuring Naboth's execution, she secured the vineyard for Ahab, demonstrating a chilling disregard for justice and God's law.

Perhaps the most infamous episode in Jezebel's story is her confrontation with Elijah, one of God's most fervent prophets. After the triumph at Mount Carmel, where Elijah demonstrated the power of Yahweh by calling down fire from heaven, Jezebel's reaction was not one of awe or repentance but of vengeance. Her threat to kill Elijah, as detailed in 1 Kings 19, reveals a woman undeterred by the power of God, committed to her pagan beliefs, and willing to go to any lengths to protect them.

Jezebel's end was as dramatic as her life. Predicted by the prophet Elijah and executed by Jehu, her demise was a stark reminder of the consequences of opposing God. Thrown from a window and trampled by horses, her body was left to the dogs, fulfilling the prophecy in a gruesome testament to divine justice.

Jezebel's legacy is complex. On the one hand, she is remembered as a figure of defiance, a queen who brought her own gods and influenced a king and his nation to forsake their faith. On the other, her story serves as a warning about the dangers of idolatry, the corruption of power, and the divine judgment that befalls those who oppose the will of God. Her life and actions remain a powerful narrative on the perils of allowing foreign influences and personal ambition to overshadow devotion and obedience to divine commandments.

Characteristics of the Jezebel Spirit

As we have seen, the figure of Jezebel stands as a towering archetype of manipulation and defiance against divine order in biblical lore. Her spirit, as gleaned from the ancient texts, is not confined to the historical narrative but extends its influence into contemporary contexts, manifesting in behaviors and attitudes that disrupt harmony, subvert righteousness, and challenge spiritual authority. Here, we delve into the multifaceted characteristics of the Jezebel spirit, highlighting its relevance and manifestations in modern relationships and structures.

Craftiness. Jezebel's hallmark trait was her cunning nature, exemplified in her orchestration of Naboth's death. She did not dirty her hands directly; instead, she laid a trap for Naboth, leveraging the legal system and social customs to eliminate him and seize his vineyard for Ahab. This act of indirect aggression reveals a calculating mind that employs manipulation to achieve its ends, a trait alarmingly relevant in today's societal interactions where deceit often masquerades as diplomacy.

Sexual Persuasion. The spirit of Jezebel is also characterized by its use of sexual allure as a means of control. While the biblical text does not explicitly detail Jezebel's personal use of seduction, her promotion of cults that involved sexual rites and her power over Ahab suggests a broader application of sexuality as a tool of influence. In contemporary terms, this manifests as the manipulation of relationships through sexual appeal, exploiting intimacy to sway decisions and actions away from moral and spiritual integrity.

Wickedness. Inherent in Jezebel's actions is a core of wickedness—a disposition that seeks to undermine, destroy, or corrupt. Her readiness to annihilate the prophets of Yahweh and her ruthless pursuit of Naboth's property underline a spirit devoid of compassion and righteousness. This wickedness is evident today in behaviors that prey upon the weak or vulnerable, exploiting them for personal gain or satisfaction.

Control as the Ultimate Goal. Jezebel's ultimate aim was control, particularly over the spiritual direction and leadership of Israel. Her introduction of Baal worship and suppression of Yahweh's prophets were driven by a desire to dictate the religious and moral landscape of her adopted country. The modern parallel is seen in individuals or systems that seek to dominate and manipulate, particularly in spiritual contexts, to enforce a personal agenda or belief system.

Inducing Fear and Discouragement. One of the most insidious effects of the Jezebel spirit is its capacity to instill fear and cause discouragement, particularly among spiritual leaders. Elijah's flight into the wilderness, prompted by Jezebel's death threats, exemplifies how even the staunchest faith can be shaken by targeted intimidation. Today, this tactic manifests in character assassination, public shaming, or relentless criticism designed to silence or discredit spiritual authority and moral voices.

Subtlety and Deception. Jezebel's manipulations were often cloaked in subtlety and deception, utilizing flattery and false allegiances to ensnare her targets. The modern incarnation of this trait is seen in the manipulation of truth and selective disclosure intended to mislead or entrap, often leaving victims confused about the true nature of their circumstances.

Alignment with Religious Spirit. Despite her opposition to the worship of Yahweh, Jezebel's actions were deeply entwined with the religious practices of her time, albeit in the promotion of false gods. This alignment with a religious spirit, while acting counter to genuine faith, highlights the danger of spiritual deception that uses the guise of religiosity to lead others astray.

Disorder in Family Dynamics. The influence of Jezebel's spirit extends into the realm of family, where her manipulative and controlling tendencies can foster discord and dysfunction. The biblical narrative does not delve deeply into Jezebel's role as a mother. Still, her impact on the kingdom of Israel suggests a legacy of turmoil and division—a warning mirrored in family structures where manipulation and control disrupt natural bonds and undermine healthy authority.

The characteristics of the Jezebel spirit serve as a cautionary guide, illuminating the pathways through which manipulation and control can infiltrate and erode the foundations of relationships, communities, and spiritual life. Recognizing these traits is the first step in guarding against their influence and fostering environments of genuine faith, integrity, and love.

Modern Day Manifestations of the Jezebel Spirit in Relationships

The Jezebel spirit, while ancient in its biblical origins, manifests in the modern day through behaviors that seek to manipulate, control, and undermine. Below, we explore examples where this spirit is evident in contemporary relationships, highlighting the red flags that signal its presence in women akin to Jezebel's archetype.

Consider the dynamic between Laura and Paul. Initially, Laura presented herself as the ideal partner—supportive, nurturing, and understanding. However, as their relationship progressed, Paul noticed unsettling shifts in Laura's behavior. She began to criticize Paul's decisions and friends, subtly isolating him from his support network at church. Whenever Paul expressed a desire to engage in activities independently or pursue personal goals, Laura would manipulate the situation to her advantage, citing emotional vulnerabilities or creating scenarios that necessitated his attention and care.

Laura's tactics mirrored Jezebel's manipulative control over Ahab as she slowly eroded Paul's autonomy, making her desires and needs the focal point of their relationship. Her ability to twist situations to elicit guilt or sympathy from Paul whenever he attempted to assert his independence is a modern echo of Jezebel's controlling nature.

Chloe and Andrew's relationship provides insight into how the Jezebel spirit can operate through undermining our beliefs in God. Andrew, rooted in faith, was initially drawn to Chloe's interest in God. However, as their relationship deepened, Chloe began introducing practices and beliefs that directly contradicted Andrew's spiritual convictions. She used seduction and emotional manipulation, praising Andrew for his open-mindedness when he entertained her ideas and belittling him as primitive or unsophisticated when he resisted.

Chloe's influence on Andrew reflects Jezebel's introduction of idol worship to Israel, aiming to shift his spiritual alignment to serve her preferences. Her manipulation was not just a challenge to Andrew's faith but an attempt to control and reshape his spiritual identity to align with her agenda, leveraging their emotional connection as a means of exerting influence.

Why You Should Avoid Marrying a Jezebel

Entering into a marriage or a deeply committed relationship is a decision that shapes the trajectory of one's life, influencing personal growth, spiritual journey, and the ability to lead a fulfilling and autonomous life. Marrying a person who exhibits traits akin to the biblical Jezebel carries profound risks that can lead to spiritual deviation, loss of personal autonomy, and a profound erosion of moral and personal integrity. Understanding these risks is crucial in recognizing why such a partnership can be detrimental.

Spiritual Deviation. One of the most significant dangers of aligning with a Jezebel-like partner is the potential for spiritual deviation. This spirit, characterized by manipulation and rebellion against the Word of God, can lead individuals away from their spiritual moorings. For those deeply committed to their faith in Christ, this deviation not only represents a loss of spiritual identity but also a departure from the church and beliefs that offer support and guidance. The influence of a Jezebel can subtly shift one's focus from spiritual fulfillment and obedience to God to the pursuit of desires and ambitions that contravene spiritual principles.

Loss of Leadership and Autonomy. A hallmark of the Jezebel spirit is its insidious attack on leadership and autonomy. Individuals under the sway of a Jezebel-like partner often find their ability to lead compromised in their families, communities, and personal lives. This spirit seeks to undermine and dominate, positioning itself as the de facto leader within the relationship. The result is a significant loss of autonomy, where decisions are no longer the product of mutual respect and partnership but are instead dictated by the controlling desires of the Jezebel-like partner. This dynamic stifles personal growth and can leave individuals trapped in a relationship that diminishes rather than uplifts their leadership capabilities.

Erosion of Personal and Moral Integrity. Closely tied to the loss of autonomy is the erosion of personal and moral integrity. The manipulative tactics employed by those embodying the Jezebel spirit can coerce partners into compromising their values and principles. Over time, the relentless push to conform to the 'Jezebel's agenda' can lead individuals to act in ways that betray their conscience and moral compass. This erosion of integrity is deeply damaging, impacting not only the individual's sense of self but also their relationships with others who value and depend on their moral leadership.

Impact on Leadership and Spiritual Path. For those called to leadership, whether in a church, ministry, or family context, the influence of a Jezebel-like partner can be particularly destructive. Such partners prioritize control over genuine partnership, often seeking to diminish their partner's authority and influence to elevate their own. This dynamic can severely impact an individual's ability to lead effectively, causing them to question their judgment, retreat from leadership roles, and lose respect from those who look up to them. The individual's spiritual path is also jeopardized as the controlling nature of a Jezebel-like partner diverts them from their divine calling and spiritual responsibilities.

Strategies for Avoidance and Discernment

Navigating the complex landscape of relationships requires a keen awareness of red flags and a committed approach to discernment and wisdom, especially when it comes to identifying and avoiding individuals who exhibit controlling, manipulative, and spiritually undermining behaviors. Here are strategies to empower you to recognize potentially harmful partners and make choices that align with their spiritual values and convictions.

Cultivate Spiritual Discernment. Spiritual discernment is an invaluable tool in identifying Jezebel-like traits in potential partners. This involves seeking a deeper connection with God through prayer and intercession and listening intently to the guidance of the Holy Spirit. Regularly engaging in prayer, meditation, and reflection will heighten your sensitivity to the subtle cues that signal manipulative or controlling behavior, enabling you to trust your spiritual instincts when something feels amiss.

Seek Wise Counsel. The wisdom of trusted church leaders, mentors, and counselors can provide clarity and confirmation when assessing a potential partner's character. These individuals often possess the experience and insight to recognize patterns of behavior that may be harmful. Sharing concerns and observations with them can help validate one's apprehensions and encourage a course of action that prioritizes well-being and spiritual integrity.

Prioritize Spiritual Compatibility. In choosing a life partner, prioritizing spiritual compatibility is essential. A relationship built on a shared commitment to spiritual values and convictions offers a solid foundation to withstand life's challenges. It's critical to have open and honest discussions about your faith, beliefs, and spiritual practices early in the relationship to ensure that both partners are aligned in their spiritual journey and commitments.

Educate Yourself on Red Flags. Awareness and education are vital components of avoidance. Familiarizing yourself with the characteristics of manipulative and controlling behaviors and understanding the dynamics of healthy versus unhealthy relationships can equip individuals to recognize red flags early on. Resources such as books, workshops, and seminars on relational health based on God's Word and spiritual well-being can provide valuable insights.

Set and Enforce Boundaries. Establishing clear boundaries is a powerful strategy for safeguarding your emotional and spiritual health. It's important to clearly communicate your limits and expectations and observe how potential partners respect these boundaries. A person who consistently pushes, ignores, or belittles your boundaries is likely exhibiting control tendencies that could escalate over time.

Listen to Your Inner Voice. Your inner witness often provides the first hint that something is wrong. If you feel consistently uneasy, diminished, or anxious in the presence of a potential partner, take these feelings seriously. They may be indicators of underlying dynamics incompatible with a healthy, spiritually aligned relationship.

Practice Patience. Finally, embracing patience in finding a life partner can prevent hasty decisions that lead to regret. Rushing into a relationship out of fear, loneliness, or societal pressure can blind individuals to warning signs. Allowing relationships to develop naturally over time can reveal a person's true character and intentions, ensuring that any commitment is based on fully understanding the partnership's potential for mutual growth and spiritual fulfillment.

Takeaway

The narrative of Jezebel, steeped in the rich tapestry of biblical history, serves as a compelling cautionary tale that transcends time and culture. Her story, marked by manipulation, control, and a stark departure from spiritual integrity, illuminates the dangers inherent in allowing such traits to infiltrate and dominate relationships. As we reflect on the characteristics of the Jezebel spirit and its manifestation in contemporary dynamics, several vital lessons emerge, guiding us toward healthier, more fulfilling partnerships.

Jezebel's legacy, characterized by craftiness, manipulation for control, and undermining of spiritual and moral foundations, offers a stark warning against the entanglement of individuals who exhibit similar behaviors. Her ability to sway King Ahab, leading him away from his spiritual duties and into the worship of false gods, underscores the profound impact that a partner can have on one's spiritual path and leadership role. This historical example emphasizes the necessity of vigilance and discernment in identifying and avoiding relationships that threaten to derail one's spiritual journey and personal autonomy.

In light of Jezebel's story, the call to pursue relationships founded on mutual respect, spiritual integrity, and shared values cannot be overstated. A partnership that honors each individual's autonomy encourages spiritual growth and fosters a climate of mutual support stands in stark contrast to the dynamics of control and manipulation epitomized by Jezebel. Such relationships are built on open communication, a commitment to shared spiritual and moral convictions, and a deep-seated respect for each other's unique contributions to the partnership.

Much like the ancient world, the modern landscape of relationships is not immune to the influences of control and manipulation. Recognizing the red flags associated with the Jezebel spirit—such as undue pressure to conform to another's will, attempts to isolate from supportive community and spiritual practices, and the erosion of personal integrity—is essential in steering clear of potentially harmful relationships. Through awareness, prayer, intercession, and a commitment to one's spiritual and moral values, individuals can navigate these challenges with wisdom and grace.

As we conclude this exploration of the Jezebel spirit and its relevance to modern relationships, let us be encouraged to seek partnerships that uplift and edify. In doing so, we honor God and the potential for genuine, loving connections that support our highest good.

Together, let us build a legacy of love, respect, and mutual growth that stands as a testament to the power of choosing well in matters of the heart.

Chapter 7

Don't Rush To Marry A Delilah

As God by creation made two of one, so again by marriage He made one of two.

— Tomas Adams

Delilah's entrance in the biblical accounts marks a turning point in the epic story of Samson, Israel's enigmatic judge endowed with unparalleled strength. Set against the backdrop of relentless hostilities between the Israelites and the Philistines, her story intertwines with Samson's in a narrative rich with themes of intrigue, betrayal, and the complexities of human desire. Delilah, whose name has become synonymous with seduction and treachery, steps into the limelight during a period fraught with tension, her actions weaving a pivotal thread in the tapestry of Israel's history.

The Philistines, desperate to neutralize Samson's devastating impact, devise a strategy that shifts the conflict from the battlefield to the more personal domain of love and betrayal. They enlist Delilah, a woman of beautiful allure, to discover the secret behind Samson's supernatural strength. This tactical shift from physical to psychological warfare underscores the Philistines' cunning, casting Delilah not merely as a femme fatale but as a central figure in their quest for dominance.

As this chapter unfolds, we delve into the intricate dance between Delilah and Samson, exploring the layers of her character and the motivations that drive her to betray the man who loves her. Through this lens, we're invited to reflect on the broader implications of their story—on the dangers of misplaced trust, the vulnerability of the human heart, and the profound impact our relationships can have on our fate. In the saga of Samson and Delilah, we find a narrative that resonates across millennia, a red flag that speaks to the enduring struggle between spiritual integrity and the seductions that seek to undermine it.

Delilah's Pact with the Philistines

In the shadowed corridors of ancient power plays, Delilah finds herself at the center of a clandestine pact that would etch her name in the annals of infamy. Wearied by their fruitless endeavors against Samson's might, the Philistine lords craft a scheme steeped in guile and desperation. They approach Delilah with a proposition laced with silver—a fortune in exchange for the enigma of Samson's invincibility.

The sum they offer, eleven hundred pieces of silver from each lord, is a testament to their urgency and a reflection of the immense value they place on Samson's downfall. This bounty promises wealth beyond imagining and a transformation of Delilah's social standing, catapulting her from the margins to the echelons of influence and power.

Delilah's motivations in this web of intrigue are complex, mirroring the multifaceted nature of temptation itself. Perhaps the allure of wealth entices her, the shimmering promise of silver enough to eclipse any moral reservations. Or it is the intoxicating prospect of acclaim, of being the woman who felled the indomitable Samson, that seduces her.

In her calculus, the rewards of betrayal dwarf the bonds of affection, revealing a pragmatism that is as chilling as it is calculating. Delilah's decision to align herself with the Philistines underscores a timeless narrative of ambition, where the ends justify the means, and loyalty is but a pawn in the greater game of personal advancement.

As we delve into the story of Delilah's pact with the Philistines, we're invited to reflect on the enduring nature of human temptation. Her story serves as a canvas, painting a portrait of the lengths individuals might go when faced with the dual sirens of wealth and fame. It is a tale that resonates through ages, a cautionary narrative that warns of the perils lurking when one's moral compass is swayed by the glittering allure of personal gain.

Modern Day Delilah's

The archetype of Delilah finds its threads interwoven with the fabric of today's world, manifesting through manipulation and seduction that stray not far from her ancient playbook. These modern-day Delilahs, with their strategies rooted in the timeless arts of persuasion and control, navigate the complexities of relationships with a cunning that belies their motives, revealing the multifaceted ways Delilah's spirit persists through the ages.

Imagine Sarah, a woman who, much like Delilah, uses her understanding of her partner, Michael's, vulnerabilities to her advantage. Michael, a man deeply committed to God, finds himself entranced by Sarah's apparent interest in spiritual matters. However, Sarah's engagement in these discussions is not driven by a genuine quest for spiritual growth but is a calculated effort to steer Michael away from his convictions.

She subtly challenges the core beliefs that Michael holds dear, suggesting that his commitment to certain doctrines is outdated and restrictive. Over time, Michael compromises on values he once deemed non-negotiable, all in the name of love and unity, not realizing that he's being led away from the very foundations of his faith.

Then there's Rachel, a figure who, under the guise of love, seeks to pull Joshua away from his spiritual commitments. Aware of Joshua's dedication to his church and ministry, Rachel initially presents herself as supportive. Yet, her support gradually morphs into a tool of seduction aimed at diminishing Joshua's involvement in church activities and ministry work, claiming it takes away from their time together. Her insistence is wrapped in the language of love but is, in essence, a ploy to isolate Joshua from his spiritual support system and commitments. Enamored by Rachel and desiring to please her, Joshua begins to neglect his duties and the spiritual disciplines that once shaped his character.

The Danger of Marrying a Delilah

Embarking on a relationship with someone who mirrors the characteristics of Delilah poses significant threats to one's spiritual journey, personal integrity, and the potential to lead effectively. Such relationships, marked by manipulation and deceit, can derail an individual from their God-given path, leading to profound spiritual disorientation and moral compromise.

Erosion of Spiritual Convictions. At the heart of the danger is the gradual erosion of spiritual convictions. Individuals like Delilah, through their manipulative tactics, can subtly influence their partners to prioritize their relationship over their relationship with God. This shift may not be abrupt but rather a slow drift away from spiritual disciplines, church, and ministry commitments that once held central importance. The consequence is a weakening of faith, where one's spiritual anchor in God becomes replaced by an unhealthy attachment to the relationship.

Compromise of Personal Integrity. Delilah-like figures often lead their partners into compromising situations that contradict their values and principles. The seduction into making choices that conflict with one's moral compass can have lasting effects on personal integrity. The compromise often starts small, with seemingly inconsequential decisions, but can escalate to more significant betrayals of one's own standards and the expectations of those who look up to them. This slippery slope can result in a loss of self-respect and the respect of peers, family, and community.

Undermining Leadership Potential. For those called to lead, be it in ministry, community, or family, a relationship with a Delilah figure can severely undermine their ability to lead with authority and conviction. Leadership, particularly spiritual leadership, requires a foundation of trust, consistency, and moral clarity. When these are compromised, one's credibility and capacity to guide others towards truth and righteousness are diminished. The manipulative partner's influence can lead to decisions that prioritize personal gain or appeasement over the welfare of those being led, eroding trust and undermining the leader's effectiveness.

Identifying A Delilah

Navigating the complexities of relationships demands wisdom and discernment, particularly in identifying individuals who may lead us away from God's path. In understanding the red flags that indicate a Delilah-like character, Scripture offers invaluable insights for recognizing potential dangers in a relationship. Reflecting on the biblical narrative of Samson and Delilah, along with other scriptural principles, can guide us in identifying the warning signs of a partner who may not have our best spiritual interests at heart.

Focus on Self-Interest. A critical warning sign of a Delilah is a pronounced focus on self-interest. This trait manifests in actions and concerns that are overwhelmingly self-centered, with little regard for their partner's needs, feelings, or spiritual well-being. Proverbs 31:30 warns, *"Charm is deceptive, and beauty is fleeting; but a woman who fears the LORD is to be praised."* (NIV) This verse encourages us to look beyond surface-level qualities and assess whether a person's life reflects a fear of the Lord or an overarching focus on themselves.

Manipulation of Weaknesses. Another hallmark of a 'Delilah' is the manipulation of weaknesses. This involves exploiting a partner's vulnerabilities for personal gain and maintaining control in the relationship. Samson's downfall was precipitated by Delilah's manipulation of his trust and love (Judges 16:4-21). Similarly, 2 Timothy 3:6-7 warns against those who *"creep into households and make captives of gullible women loaded down with sins, led away by various lusts, always learning and never able to come to the knowledge of the truth."* (NIV) Observing if someone uses knowledge of your weaknesses to manipulate or control you is crucial in discerning their character.

Persistence in Deceit. A persistent effort to deceive or manipulate, even in the face of evidence revealing their actions, is a significant red flag. Despite his initial refusals, Delilah's repeated attempts to uncover the source of Samson's strength demonstrate a relentless pursuit of her agenda (Judges 16:10-16). Jesus' admonition in Matthew 7:15-16 to *"Beware of false prophets, who come to you in sheep's clothing but inwardly are ravenous wolves.* (ESV) *You will recognize them by their fruits,"* underscores the importance of evaluating the consistent fruit of a person's actions and words. Continuous deceit and manipulation, particularly that which seeks to pull you away from your convictions and relationship with God, should not be overlooked.

Strategies for Avoidance and Discernment

The biblical narrative of Samson and Delilah offers a profound lesson on the perils of entanglement with individuals who exhibit behaviors aimed at manipulation and control. Several strategies rooted in spiritual discernment and wisdom can be employed to avoid such entanglements.

Spiritual Discernment. The first and most vital strategy is cultivating spiritual discernment, a gift from God that enables believers to perceive and distinguish between the spirit of truth and the spirit of deception. James 1:5 encourages us to seek wisdom from God, who gives generously to all without finding fault. Engaging in prayer, meditation on Scripture, and fasting are practices that enhance our spiritual discernment. As we draw closer to God and immerse ourselves in His Word, we become more attuned to His voice and guidance, enabling us to recognize the motives and intentions of those we engage with.

Seeking Wise Counsel. Proverbs 12:15 states, *"The way of fools seems right to them, but the wise listen to advice."* (NIV) In matters of the heart, seeking the counsel of spiritually mature individuals—pastors, mentors, or trusted friends grounded in their faith—can provide clarity and perspective that we might miss due to our emotions or personal biases. These individuals can offer biblical advice, pray with us, and help us evaluate the character and intentions of a potential partner through the lens of Scripture.

Aligning with Partners Who Share and Respect One's Values. 2 Corinthians 6:14 warns against being unequally yoked with unbelievers, highlighting the potential for conflict and spiritual discord in such unions. It's essential to seek a partner who not only professes faith but whose life bears fruit in keeping with repentance (Matthew 3:8). Shared values and mutual respect for each other's spiritual journey are foundational to a relationship that honors God. Conversations about faith, values, future goals, and priorities should be part of the early stages of a relationship, providing insight into whether a potential partner is truly aligned with one's spiritual and moral convictions.

Personal Boundaries. Establishing and maintaining personal boundaries is another critical strategy. Boundaries help define what is acceptable and what isn't in a relationship, protecting us from manipulation and control. Galatians 5:1 encourages us to stand firm in the freedom Christ has given us and not to be burdened again by the yoke of slavery. Communicating these boundaries clearly and early on—and observing how they are respected—indicates a partner's respect for you and your values.

Continuous Self-Reflection and Growth. Lastly, personal spiritual growth and self-reflection are indispensable. Understanding our vulnerabilities and weaknesses—and working on them through prayer and personal development—can decrease the likelihood of falling prey to manipulative behaviors. Psalm 139:23-24's plea for God to search our hearts and lead us in the way everlasting is a model for the introspective work necessary to grow in discernment and wisdom.

Takeaway

In concluding our exploration of the narrative of Delilah within the biblical context, we revisit the profound lessons her story imparts on contemporary relationships. Delilah's tale, as presented in the Scriptures, is a compelling illustration of the perils that accompany relationships founded on deceit, manipulation, and a disregard for spiritual integrity. Her actions, motivated by self-interest and the promise of gain, led to the downfall of Samson, a man chosen by God to lead and deliver Israel.

This narrative underscores the critical importance of vigilance, wisdom, and discernment in selecting a life partner. Proverbs 4:23 admonishes us to *"guard your heart above all else, for it determines the course of your life"* (NLT). The story of Samson and Delilah reminds us that the heart is susceptible to deception, particularly when enticed by superficial allurements that distract from spiritual and moral incongruities.

As believers, we are called to pursue relationships anchored in mutual respect, honesty, and a shared commitment to spiritual values. 2 Corinthians 6:14 warns against being unequally yoked with unbelievers, highlighting the potential for spiritual discord and compromise. Instead, we are encouraged to seek partners who profess faith and whose lives reflect a genuine relationship with God, as evidenced by their actions, decisions, and the fruit of the Spirit in their lives (Galatians 5:22-23).

The cautionary tale of Delilah invites us to reflect deeply on the qualities we value in a partner. It prompts a consideration of character over charm, substance over surface, and spiritual compatibility over fleeting attraction. In navigating the complexities of relationships, let us be guided by the wisdom of Proverbs 3:5-6, which instructs us to *"Trust in the Lord with all your heart and lean not on your own understanding; in all your ways submit to him, and he will make your paths straight."* (NIV)

May we seek the Lord's guidance, wisdom, and discernment

in forming relationships that honor Him and foster mutual growth in faith. Let the story of Delilah serve as a reminder to prioritize spiritual integrity and godly character in choosing a life partner. May our relationships be a testament to God's grace, love, and faithfulness as we build lives and families that reflect His glory and purpose.

Chapter 8

Don't Rush to Marry Lot's Wife

Love is patient and kind; love does not envy or boast; it is not arrogant or rude. It does not insist on its own way; it is not irritable or resentful; it does not rejoice at wrongdoing, but rejoices with the truth. Love bears all things, believes all things, hopes all things, endures all things.

— 1 Corinthians 13:4-7 (ESV)

The story of Lot's wife is a poignant testament to the severe consequences of disobedience and the allure of worldly attachments. Situated within the narrative of Sodom and Gomorrah's impending doom, her tale unfolds at a juncture of divine grace and judgment, offering a profound lesson on the spiritual and moral exigencies of faith.

As dawn crept over the horizon, casting a pale light on the wicked cities of Sodom and Gomorrah, divine messengers dispatched by the Lord arrived with a decree of destruction and a message of salvation. Lot, a man caught between the righteousness of his uncle Abraham and the depravity of his surroundings, found himself at the epicenter of a divine intervention designed to preserve his family from the catastrophic judgment about to rain down upon the cities of the plain.

The narrative, chronicled in Genesis 19:15-26, captures a moment of mercy amidst impending wrath. In their celestial mercy, the angels grasp the hands of Lot, his wife, and their two daughters, urging them to flee the corruption that enveloped their home. *"Escape for your life! Do not look behind you nor stay anywhere in the plain. Escape to the mountains, lest you be destroyed,"* they warned, a directive imbued with both compassion and command.

Yet, as they hastened from the city, a heart-wrenching drama unfolded. Lot's wife, whose name history has been left unrecorded, became emblematic of a profound spiritual struggle. A visceral compulsion overcame her as the divine wrath began its purging fire. Whether driven by a longing glance at her former life, a pang of loss for her worldly possessions, or disbelief in the divine promise, she looked back. At that moment, she transformed from a fleeing survivor to a pillar of salt—a permanent monument to the cost of disobedience and the fatal pull of material attachment.

This act of looking back was not merely a physical turning but symbolized a deeper, spiritual resistance to fully relinquishing a past marred by sin and corruption. The angels' command to not look back was a test of faith, a directive to leave behind the old life of sin and embrace a future ordained by God.

Lot's wife's inability to forsake her past, even in the face of divine deliverance, is a warning for all believers. It underscores the vital importance of obedience, the danger of nostalgia for sinful ways, and the catastrophic consequences of allowing worldly desires to supersede divine directives.

The Significance of Disobedience

The act of disobedience by Lot's wife, as she cast that fateful glance back towards the burning cities of Sodom and Gomorrah, stands as a stark emblem of the perilous consequences that follow when divine commands are flouted. Her transformation into a pillar of salt is not merely a punitive response to a singular act of defiance but serves as a profound allegory for the spiritual ramifications of yearning for a life steeped in sin, symbolizing the irreversible consequences of choosing worldly attachments over obedience to God.

While brief in its biblical recounting, this episode encapsulates a profound lesson on the gravity of disobedience. The instruction of God, issued in the context of divine mercy and deliverance, was imbued with the urgency and gravity of the situation. Yet, Lot's wife's decision to look back reveals a deeper, more insidious struggle—a reluctance to fully relinquish her past and a resistance to the transformative call of God.

Her disobedience serves as a poignant reminder of the human propensity to cling to familiar sin and the material comforts of this world, even when they are clearly identified as destructive. It highlights the spiritual danger inherent in allowing our hearts to remain attached to this life's temporal pleasures and possessions to the point where they impede our obedience to God and endanger our spiritual well-being.

The consequences of her action extend far beyond the personal tragedy of Lot's wife; they serve as a cautionary tale for all believers. The instant transformation into a pillar of salt vividly illustrates the finality and severity of judgment that can result from disobedience to God's commands. This narrative element underscores the biblical principle that disobedience not only separates us from the protective grace of God but also solidifies our fate in the face of impending judgment.

Moreover, the story of Lot's wife resonates with the teachings of Jesus Christ, who admonished His followers to remember her as a warning against the perils of looking back or holding onto one's life in the face of a divine call to salvation and transformation. In Luke 17:32, the simple yet profound command, "Remember Lot's wife," serves as a somber reminder of the cost of prioritizing earthly life and possessions over the eternal life offered by Christ.

In reflecting upon the significance of disobedience exemplified by Lot's wife, we are called to examine our own lives for areas where attachment to the world might hinder our complete obedience to God. Her story urges us to let go of the sinful past and worldly entanglements, to embrace wholeheartedly the path of righteousness laid out by God, lest we, too, become emblematic of the tragic cost of disobedience.

Considering the profound lesson of disobedience illustrated by Lot's wife, it becomes imperative on the journey to finding a life partner to introspectively assess how the woman's attachments to worldly desires and pleasures may obstruct her obedience to God's will. Her narrative is a compelling call to action, urging us to relinquish our grip on past transgressions and material obsessions and wholeheartedly pursue the righteous path

God has delineated for us. This is especially crucial in marriage, where the choice of a spouse should align with our spiritual values and God's plan for our lives.

Modern-Day Reflections: The Allure of the World

In today's fast-paced, materialistically driven society, the account of Lot's wife is a stark reminder of the perils accompanying a deep-seated attachment to the world and its fleeting pleasures. This biblical narrative resonates profoundly with the challenges that modern believers face as they navigate through a culture saturated with worldly allurements that threaten to compromise their spiritual integrity.

The scripture in 1 John 2:15-17 admonishes believers not to love the world or the things in it, warning that the love of the Father is not in those who do. This passage starkly delineates the dichotomy between godly and worldly values, cautioning against the lust of the flesh, the lust of the eyes, and the pride of life—all of which are not from the Father but are of the world. In essence, this scripture encourages us to detach from worldly possessions and accolades, emphasizing that the world and its desires are passing away, but those who do the will of God live forever.

Furthermore, Jesus' exhortation to "Remember Lot's wife" in Luke 17:32 serves as a poignant reminder of the consequences of looking back—of longing for a life left behind when God calls us forward. This reference is embedded in a discourse about the end times, where Christ warns of the suddenness of His coming and the urgency of being prepared, unencumbered by earthly ties. It underscores the critical importance of prioritizing eternal values over temporal gains, urging believers to live in a state of readiness, their lives marked by a godly detachment from worldly enticements.

In reflecting on the story of Lot's wife in contemporary life, we are invited to examine our hearts and lifestyles. Are there areas where the allure of the world is drawing their focus away from God? Are the choices we are making in pursuit of a spouse, career, or lifestyle in alignment with God's eternal values, or are they rooted in worldly desires? The story of Lot's wife serves as a sobering call to assess and align one's priorities, ensuring that our lives are built on the unshakeable foundation of God's eternal Kingdom rather than the shifting sands of worldly acclaim and possessions.

In the quest for a life partner, this reflection becomes crucial. It challenges us to seek companionship not merely based on worldly standards of wealth, beauty, or status but on spiritual harmony and shared commitment to living out God's purpose. For women of God striving to navigate life's choices, the story of Lot's wife is a timeless beacon, guiding you towards decisions that honor God, foster spiritual growth, and contribute to your ultimate well-being in Christ.

Identifying Lot's Wife Today

In the contemporary quest for companionship, discerning the characteristics of a "Lot's wife" mentality in potential partners is crucial for those committed to a life of spiritual integrity. This archetype, drawn from the biblical narrative, represents individuals whose priorities are misaligned with the values of faith, showcasing an excessive love for the world and its material comforts at the expense of spiritual depth and commitment. Key characteristics to watch for include:

Excessive Worldliness: An overriding preoccupation with acquiring wealth, status, and material possessions. This trait is evident in individuals who value what is temporal over what is eternal, often pursuing lifestyle choices heavily influenced by societal standards rather than spiritual convictions.

Disregard for Spiritual Commitments: A marked indifference or even resistance to spiritual practices and values. This may manifest as a reluctance to pray, study scripture, or participate in church activities, indicating a heart not fully surrendered to God.

Materialism as a Predilection: A strong inclination towards materialism, where happiness and fulfillment are sought in physical comforts and possessions rather than in a relationship with God and in serving others. This mindset often leads to a cycle of never-ending desire for more, which can be detrimental to both individual and relational spiritual health.

For men contemplating marriage, these traits serve as red flags, signaling the potential for a relationship that could veer off the spiritual path God intends for His followers. It's essential to approach relationships with discernment, seeking partners who not only profess faith but also demonstrate a life that bears fruit in keeping with that profession.

Warning signs include conversations devoid of spiritual depth, a lack of interest in discussing or participating in faith-based activities, and a lifestyle prioritizing luxury and status over generosity and humility. Observing how a potential partner values and manages their resources can also provide insight into their heart's true treasure.

The Danger of Marrying Lot's Wife

Marrying someone who embodies the characteristics of Lot's wife poses significant spiritual, emotional, and relational challenges. This union can profoundly affect one's faith, leading to potential derailment from the path God has intended. In a modern context, this translates to marrying individuals whose priorities and values are misaligned with those of the Kingdom of God.

Spiritual Ramifications: A relationship with a wife prioritizing worldly gains over spiritual values can lead to a weakened faith and a diminished relationship with God. The spiritual disconnect affects personal communion with God and can create an environment where spiritual disciplines and growth are neglected. The danger lies in the subtle shift from God-centric living towards a life that glorifies materialism and self-satisfaction, reminiscent of Lot's wife's fatal glance back.

Emotional Consequences: Emotionally, being with a wife who lacks spiritual depth and commitment can lead to feelings of isolation and spiritual loneliness. The emotional bond in a marriage is significantly strengthened when both partners share a common faith and vision for their life together. Without this shared spiritual foundation, the emotional intimacy necessary for a fulfilling relationship can be compromised, leading to dissatisfaction and a sense of incompleteness.

Relational Impacts: Relationally, the disparity in values and priorities can create ongoing conflicts and misunderstandings.

Decisions about finances, parenting, lifestyle choices, and social engagements can become battlegrounds when the wife's worldview is anchored in pursuing worldly pleasures and achievements while the husband seeks to live according to God's will. These conflicts can hinder the couple's ability to function as a unified team, pursuing common goals and supporting each other's spiritual growth.

The apostle Paul warns against being "unequally yoked" with unbelievers (2 Corinthians 6:14), emphasizing the challenges and conflicts that arise when foundational beliefs and values diverge. Marrying someone with the characteristics of Lot's wife—a metaphor for worldliness and disobedience—can lead to a life of spiritual compromise, where one's ability to live out one's faith is continually challenged by one's partner's worldly inclinations.

For believers, the decision to marry should be approached with prayerful consideration, seeking a partner who not only professes faith but whose life bears witness to that profession. The goal is to build a relationship that glorifies God, where both partners encourage each other towards deeper faith, greater love, and a life that bears fruit in keeping with the teachings of Christ. In doing so, they safeguard their relationship from the dangers associated with marrying someone who, like Lot's wife, looks back longingly at the world instead of looking forward to the promises of God.

Strategies for Avoidance and Discernment

In navigating the complexities of relationships and marriage, believers are called to exercise wisdom, spiritual discernment, and a reliance on God's guidance to avoid forming unions with individuals who exhibit traits reminiscent of Lot's wife. Here are strategic approaches to ensure alignment with God's will in selecting a wife:

Cultivate Spiritual Discernment: Spiritual discernment is crucial in recognizing the characteristics of potential partners who may lead one away from God's path. Believers must pray for the Holy Spirit's guidance to perceive beyond surface appearances and for wisdom to understand the actual spiritual state and intentions of those they consider for marriage. *"But the natural man does not receive the things of the Spirit of God, for they are foolishness to him; nor can he know them, because they are spiritually discerned"* 1 Corinthians 2:14. (KJV)

Prayerful Consideration: Engage in earnest prayer, seeking God's wisdom and direction in choosing a wife. Ask God to reveal any warning signs and to provide peace and clarity about the relationship. James 1:5 promises, *"If any of you lacks wisdom, let him ask of God, who gives to all liberally and without reproach, and it will be given to him."* (KJV)

Seek Godly Counsel: Consult with spiritually mature individuals such as pastors, mentors, or trusted Christian friends who can offer biblical advice and insights into the relationship. Proverbs 15:22 states, *"Without counsel, plans go awry, but in the multitude of counselors they are established."* (KJV) The perspectives of those who are spiritually grounded can help identify potential issues and confirm if the relationship aligns with God's will.

Evaluate Shared Values and Priorities: Assess whether both you and your potential wife prioritize your relationship with God and demonstrate a commitment to living according to biblical principles. Shared spiritual goals, values, and practices are foundational to a godly marriage. Amos 3:3 poses the question, *"Can two walk together, unless they are agreed?"* (KJV) A partner who shares your dedication to Christ will support mutual spiritual growth and a Christ-centered life.

Observe Their Fruit: Jesus taught that *"every good tree bears good fruit, but a bad tree bears bad fruit"* (Matthew 7:17). Observe the fruit of the Spirit in their life (Galatians 5:22-23) and their behavior in various circumstances. Actions often speak louder than words, and a consistent life of faith and obedience to God is a strong indicator of their spiritual health.

Guard Your Heart: Proverbs 4:23 advises, *"Keep your heart with all diligence, for out of it spring the issues of life."* (KJV) Be cautious not to rush into emotional attachments before assessing the spiritual compatibility and long-term potential of the relationship.

By implementing these strategies, you can navigate the selection of a life partner with wisdom and discernment, ensuring your choice honors God and fosters a relationship built on mutual faith, love, and respect.

Takeaway

As we reflect on the story of Lot's wife, several vital lessons emerge, resonating with profound significance for believers today, especially in relationships and marriage. Her story, though succinct, encapsulates the peril of allowing worldly attachments and desires to overshadow our obedience and commitment to God. This narrative serves as a powerful reminder of the importance of prioritizing our spiritual integrity above all else.

Shared Spiritual Values: The cornerstone of any relationship that seeks to honor God is the foundation of shared spiritual values. Believers are called to seek partners who not only profess faith but whose lives bear witness to their commitment to Christ. This shared spiritual journey is crucial for navigating the challenges of life together, fostering a relationship that glorifies God and edifies each other.

Mutual Respect and Honor: Mutual respect forms the bedrock of a healthy, godly relationship. It entails honoring one another above oneself (Romans 12:10), listening to each other's perspectives, and valuing each other's well-being. This mutual respect is fundamental in maintaining a relationship that reflects the love and grace of Christ.

Commitment to God's Purpose: A partnership centered around a joint commitment to fulfilling God's purpose for their lives is poised for spiritual growth and impact. Couples should seek to discern and embrace God's calling for their union, whether in ministry, parenting, or serving their community. This shared commitment to God's purpose strengthens the bond between them and extends the Kingdom of God through their united efforts.

In summarizing the lessons from Lot's wife, believers are reminded of the transient nature of this world and the eternal significance of our choices, particularly in the realm of relationships. The allure of the world, with its fleeting pleasures and material gains, pales in comparison to the eternal joy and fulfillment found in a life lived in obedience to God.

Therefore, as we navigate the path to finding a life partner, let us do so with prayerful discernment, seeking the Lord's guidance at every step. Let us prioritize spiritual compatibility, striving to build relationships that withstand the test of time and flourish in the light of God's love and purpose. May our relationships be a testament to the transformative power of a life surrendered to Christ, inspiring others to seek the same depth of spiritual intimacy and commitment.

Let the story of Lot's wife serve as a sobering reminder to "Remember Lot's wife" (Luke 17:32), not merely as a historical caution but as a present-day guide to making choices that align with our heavenly calling. May our relationships and marriages reflect the beauty of Christ's love, leading us closer to Him and each other as we journey together toward our eternal home.

Chapter 9

Don't Rush to Marry a Potiphar's Wife

The best love is the kind that awakens the soul and makes us reach for more, that plants a fire in our hearts and brings peace to our minds. And that's what you've given me. That's what I'd hoped to give you forever.

— Nicholas Sparks

Within the pages of Genesis, we encounter a figure whose actions have echoed through centuries as a warning against the perils of temptation and moral compromise: Potiphar's wife. Her story, intertwined with that of Joseph, a young man of exceptional faith and integrity, presents a compelling tableau of the challenges that confront those who strive to live righteously in the face of worldly allure.

Joseph, having been sold into slavery by his own brothers, finds himself in Egypt, in the service of Potiphar, an officer of

Pharaoh. Here, amidst the trials of bondage, Joseph's steadfastness to God and his principles shines brightly, earning him favor in the eyes of his master. However, this favor does not shield him from the trials to come; it merely sets the stage for a test of character that would define his spiritual legacy.

Genesis 39:7-10 narrates the relentless advances made by Potiphar's wife towards Joseph. Despite her high social standing and the power she wielded within her household, she finds herself captivated by Joseph's comeliness and form. In a brazen overture that defies the sanctity of marriage and virtue, she commands Joseph to lie with her.

Joseph's response to this proposition is a testament to his unwavering commitment to righteousness. With a resolve born of his deep reverence for God, he refuses her advances, articulating the gravity of such a sin not just against his master but, more importantly, against God Himself. Joseph's refusal is not merely a denial of a momentary temptation; it is a declaration of his allegiance to a moral code that transcends personal gain or loss.

This case study of Joseph's encounter with Potiphar's wife is a profound lesson in the face of temptation. Despite the potential consequences of such a refusal, Joseph's ability to resist her propositions stands as a model of virtue and faithfulness. His story illuminates the stark contrast between moral integrity and the downfall that awaits those who succumb to the seductive allure of sin.

As we delve deeper into this narrative, we find that the dilemma faced by Joseph is not relegated to the annals of history. It is a vivid representation of the moral and spiritual dilemmas that continue to confront believers in their daily lives. The figure of Potiphar's wife embodies the myriad temptations that beckon with the promise of pleasure or gain yet lead only to spiritual ruin.

Joseph's resolute stance against Potiphar's wife is a powerful example of navigating the complex interplay of morals, temptation, and duty. His story is not merely a recounting of a historical event but a guidepost for all who seek to maintain their spiritual integrity in a world brimming with moral challenges. Through Joseph's example, we are called to reflect on our own responses to the temptations that we face and to draw strength from his unwavering commitment to God's righteous path.

The Character of Potiphar's Wife

Potiphar's wife stands as a stark embodiment of temptation within the biblical narrative, her character serving as a cautionary emblem of the seductive allurements that beckon souls away from the path of righteousness. Her aggressive pursuit of Joseph, marked by a manipulation that seeks to subvert his integrity, casts her as an archetype of worldly temptation, one that is not merely content to tempt but seeks to ensnare and dominate.

This narrative invites us to contemplate the nuanced dimensions of temptation, as personified by Potiphar's wife. Her actions are not merely those of personal desire; they are reflective of a deeper, more insidious attempt to undermine the spiritual and moral foundations of another. Through her, the Scripture vividly illustrates how temptation often cloaks itself in the guise of harmlessness or even desirability, only to reveal its true nature when one is most vulnerable.

The story of Potiphar's wife and Joseph provides profound scriptural insights into the nature of temptation. James 1:14-15 teaches, *"But each person is tempted when he is lured and enticed by his own desire. Then desire when it has conceived gives birth to sin, and sin when it is fully grown brings forth death."* (ESV) In this light, Potiphar's wife's attempts can be seen as the embodiment of such luring and enticing, a vivid illustration of how desires, when left unchecked, can lead one to actions that directly oppose God's Word.

Her relentless pursuit of Joseph underlines a pivotal biblical theme: the call to resist not just the act of sin but the very enticements that lead to it. The narrative underscores that resisting temptation is not merely about avoiding adverse outcomes but about affirming one's allegiance to God's commandments and honoring the sanctity of commitments made before God.

Moreover, Potiphar's wife's character invites believers to reflect on the seductive nature of sin, how it often presents itself through outward appearances and immediate gratifications that promise fulfillment but ultimately lead to spiritual and moral bankruptcy. 1 Peter 5:8 admonishes, *"Be sober-minded; be watchful. Your adversary the devil prowls around like a roaring lion, seeking someone to devour."* (ESV) In this context, Potiphar's wife can be seen as an agent of such prowling, a reminder that the devil often uses human agents to achieve his ends.

Her actions, therefore, serve as a critical lesson for believers: to discern and resist the subtle machinations of temptation that threaten to derail your spiritual journey. It is a call to vigilance, to guard one's heart and mind against the deceptions that masquerade as innocuous or even beneficial, reminding us that the true measure of our faith is often found in our capacity to resist what the world offers in favor of what God commands.

In contemplating the character of Potiphar's wife, we are invited to a deeper understanding of the spiritual warfare that underpins our earthly journey. While rooted in ancient times, her story resonates with timeless relevance, urging us to steadfastness, discernment, and an unwavering commitment to the values and virtues that define a life lived in obedience to God.

Modern Day Sugar Mommies

In the contemporary landscape, the phenomenon of "sugar mommies" mirrors the seductive allure once wielded by Potiphar's wife, albeit under a modern guise. This dynamic, where older, financially secure women offer material benefits in exchange for companionship or romantic involvement with younger men, echoes the biblical narrative's warnings against yielding to material gain and the deceptive comfort of illicit relationships.

The allure of sugar mommies lies not merely in the financial stability they promise but in the deeper, more insidious suggestion that love and security can be commodified. Young men, often at a crossroads in their lives, may find the immediate gratification of such arrangements tempting, overlooking the spiritual emptiness and relational instability that such dependencies foster. The moral implications of engaging in these dynamics are profound, challenging individuals to reflect on the values and principles that guide their lives.

Scripture provides a rich tapestry of wisdom on these matters, urging believers to seek treasures that are not of this world. Matthew 6:24 reminds us, *"No one can serve two masters. For either he will hate the one and love the other, or he will be devoted to the one and despise the other. You cannot serve God and money."* (ESV) This verse encapsulates the heart of the dilemma posed by sugar mommy relationships: the impossible attempt to reconcile the pursuit of material gain with a life led by spiritual conviction.

Moreover, the concept of sugar mommies, much like the story of Potiphar's wife, serves as a cautionary tale about the illusion of companionship. True companionship, rooted in mutual respect, shared values, and a commitment to growth, stands in stark contrast to relationships founded on transactional dynamics. 1 Corinthians 15:33 warns, *"Do not be misled: 'Bad company corrupts good character.'"* This admonition invites young men to scrutinize the nature of their relationships, recognizing that the company they keep can profoundly influence their path, character, and spiritual well-being.

Urging young men to consider the long-term consequences of such relationships, the discussion invites a deeper contemplation of what it means to live a life aligned with God's purposes. It challenges the notion that wealth and comfort are the ultimate goals, instead proposing a vision of life where spiritual integrity, meaningful connections, and the pursuit of divine calling are paramount.

In reflecting on modern-day sugar mommies, young men are encouraged to discern the temporary pleasures and gains these relationships offer against the backdrop of eternal values and truths. It is a call to prioritize not what the world offers but what God promises—a life of purpose, dignity, and fulfillment that transcends the fleeting allure of material comforts and illicit enticements.

Questions for Self-Examination

In the journey toward understanding the nature of our relationships and the moral fabric that binds them, young men are invited to embark on a path of self-examination, drawing inspiration from the resilience and spiritual integrity demonstrated by Joseph in the face of Potiphar's wife's advances. This introspection is not merely an academic exercise but a profound spiritual inquiry into the heart's true desires and the soul's alignment with God's will.

The process of self-examination involves a series of pivotal questions that probe the depths of one's character and the nature of one's relationships:

What are my vulnerabilities? Identifying personal weaknesses and areas of temptation is crucial in guarding against potential falls into sin. It's about understanding what draws one's heart away from God and into the embrace of worldly pleasures.

How do I measure the integrity of my relationships? Reflecting on the foundations upon which relationships are built—is it mutual respect, shared faith, and values, or are they predicated on the shifting sands of material gain and superficial allurements?

Do my relationships bring me closer to God? Evaluating

whether interactions and connections foster spiritual growth or lead to spiritual stagnation. It's assessing if a relationship encourages the pursuit of God's Kingdom or anchors the soul to the temporal realm.

Am I prioritizing God's will in my life? Consider whether relationship choices align with God's purpose and calling. It's about ensuring that the pursuit of companionship does not eclipse the overarching goal of living a life that honors God.

Scriptural guidance for discerning the character of potential partners comes from 2 Corinthians 6:14, which admonishes, *"Do not be unequally yoked with unbelievers. For what partnership has righteousness with lawlessness? Or what fellowship has light with darkness?"* (ESV) This verse underscores the importance of shared faith and values, reminding young men that spiritual harmony is fundamental to the health and integrity of a relationship.

The questions posed for self-examination, and the scriptural references provided serve as tools for young men to navigate the terrain of relationships with wisdom and discernment. They are a call to prioritize not the fleeting enticements of the world but the eternal promises of God—a call to seek partners who share a commitment to faith, integrity, and the pursuit of a life that glorifies the Creator. In doing so, they safeguard their spiritual journey and lay the foundation for relationships that reflect the depth, purity, and enduring love that God desires for His children.

The Dangers of Entering into a Relationship with Potiphar's Wife

Entering into a relationship with a figure reminiscent of Potiphar's wife carries many dangers beyond the immediate allure of material benefits or superficial attraction. Such relationships pose significant spiritual, emotional, and societal risks that can profoundly compromise one's faith, integrity, and envisioned future. The Bible offers timeless wisdom and cautionary guidance that remains acutely relevant for navigating these treacherous waters.

The spiritual peril of aligning oneself with a "Potiphar's wife" cannot be understated. Scripture vividly illustrates the consequences of being unequally yoked with individuals who do not share a commitment to God's principles. A relationship with someone who embodies the manipulative and deceitful traits of Potiphar's wife threatens to pull one away from the path of righteousness, ensnaring the believer in a web of moral compromise and spiritual estrangement from God.

Moreover, the emotional toll of such entanglements cannot be overlooked. The heart's vulnerability to deceit and manipulation underscores the importance of vigilance in romantic pursuits. A 'Potiphar's wife' figure, with her seductive allure and hidden agendas, can lead to profound emotional turmoil and pain, leaving scars that may hinder future relationships and personal peace.

From a societal perspective, relationships predicated on imbalance, manipulation, and disregard for spiritual values often result in damaging repercussions. The disapproval and consequences of engaging in morally compromised relationships can tarnish one's reputation, disrupt familial and social bonds, and hinder professional and personal growth.

Strategies for Avoidance and Discernment

In navigating the complexities of relationships, particularly when faced with individuals who exhibit traits akin to Potiphar's wife, it is crucial for young men to employ strategies rooted in spiritual discernment and godly guidance.

The biblical narrative of Joseph not only highlights the perils of succumbing to such temptations but also offers a blueprint for maintaining integrity and faithfulness in the face of allurements. Herein lies practical advice for young men seeking to avoid the pitfalls of entanglement with characters reminiscent of Potiphar's wife:

Cultivate Spiritual Discernment: The ability to discern between right and wrong, truth and deception, comes from a deep relationship with God. Young men are encouraged to immerse themselves in prayer and meditation on God's Word, allowing the Holy Spirit to sharpen their discernment and guide their decisions.

Seek God's Guidance in Prayer: In every aspect of life, especially in matters of the heart, prayer is a powerful conduit for seeking God's will. Through prayer, young men can ask for clarity, protection from deception, and the strength to resist temptation. Philippians 4:6-7 encourages believers to present their requests to God, assuring them of peace that transcends understanding.

Embrace Godly Counsel: The wisdom of those who have walked with God and navigated similar challenges can be invaluable. Seeking advice from godly mentors, pastors, and trusted Christian friends can provide perspective, accountability, and encouragement. Proverbs 15:22 highlights the importance of such counsel, "*Plans fail for lack of counsel, but with many advisers they succeed."*

Adhere to Scriptural Wisdom: Scripture is replete with principles and precepts that guide believers in living lives that honor God, including relationships. Passages such as Ephesians 5:3 and 1 Thessalonians 4:3-5 offer guidance on maintaining purity and honoring God with one's body and relationships. Young men are urged to align their relationship standards with those outlined in Scripture, ensuring their actions reflect their commitment to Christ.

Evaluate Character Over Charm: In the allure of attraction, it's easy to overlook character flaws. Yet, 1 Samuel 16:7 reminds us that while humans look at the outward appearance, the Lord looks at the heart. Prioritizing spiritual compatibility, shared values, and a mutual commitment to God over superficial attributes can safeguard young men from entanglements with detrimental consequences.

Takeaway

The encounter between Joseph and Potiphar's wife is a powerful reminder of the virtues of godliness and the dangers of compromise. Joseph's ability to resist Potiphar's wife's advances, rooted in his fear of God and dedication to doing what is right, exemplifies the kind of spiritual integrity that believers are called to maintain in all their relationships. It highlights the significance of being anchored in your faith and values, ensuring that these guide your decisions and actions in the realm of romance and beyond.

The call is clear to young men in the journey of finding a life partner: Pursue purity, uphold integrity, and embody godliness in your relationships. Let the Word of God be your guide, and seek partners who share your commitment to Christ.

Chapter 10

Don't Rush To Marry A Michal

To be loved but not known is comforting but superficial. To be known and not loved is our greatest fear. But to be fully known and truly loved is, well, a lot like being loved by God. It is what we need more than anything. It liberates us from pretense, humbles us out of our self-righteousness, and fortifies us for any difficulty life can throw at us.

— Timothy Keller

In the vastness of biblical narratives, the story of Michal, the daughter of King Saul, emerges as a poignant saga of love entwined with the undercurrents of political intrigue and spiritual dissonance.

Entrusted to David—a humble shepherd anointed king—Michal's marriage becomes less a union of hearts and more a strategic snare set by her father. This alliance, conceived in the shadows of ulterior motives, unfolds into a story of transformation where initial love morphs into a trap, underscoring the unpredictable journey of hearts misaligned and spirits estranged.

Michal's affection for David initially shines with the promise of unity and companionship. This bond, however, bears the weight of King Saul's cunning design, aiming to ensnare David under the guise of marital bliss. Despite these covert intentions, Michal's genuine fondness for David suggests a beacon of hope for their shared future. Yet, the crucible of their bond—and Michal's spiritual alignment—reveals itself not in the quiet moments of intimacy but in the exuberant expressions of faith.

The scripture, especially within the verses of 2 Samuel 6:14-22, vividly captures a kingdom immersed in spiritual jubilation, with David's exultant dance before the Lord epitomizing his unbridled devotion. This moment of celebration before the Lord starkly contrasts with Michal's perception.

Peering through the window, she sees not a monarch in sacred worship but a figure she deems diminished by his undignified display. The heart that once harbored affection now hardens, unveiling a chasm that spans beyond mere personal grievance to touch upon the profound differences in their spiritual understandings.

Michal's reaction to David's act of worship—her scorn and confrontation—serves as a poignant reminder of the perils embedded in a partnership devoid of spiritual harmony. Her inability to perceive the eternal weight of David's gesture illuminates the tragic disconnect from her spiritual bearings. This episode of disdain, forever etched in the annals of scripture, compels a deeper contemplation on marriage's essence: a sacred covenant that transcends the union of two souls to encompass a shared journey towards God.

As the layers of Michal's narrative are delicately unraveled, her story transcends its historical and personal confines, beckoning a reflection on the essence of choosing a life partner. It heralds the critical importance of spiritual compatibility, where mutual reverence for each other's relationship with God forms the bedrock of a marriage resilient enough to weather life's storms. Through Michal's descent from love to contempt for David's spiritual exuberance, we are imparted a valuable lesson. A godly compass must invariably guide the heart in the sacred pursuit of marriage.

The episode of Michal's public rebuke of King David marks a moment of profound discord within their matrimonial harmony, laying bare the depths of their spiritual misalignment. Upon David's return, his soul ablaze with joy, Michal's response is not of shared elation but of cold disdain. This interaction, preserved in scripture, uncovers not merely a wife's critique of perceived indignity but a profound dismissal of the essence of David's faith and his consecrated role as Israel's anointed sovereign.

Her critique, masked by concerns of propriety, belies a deeper malaise—a failure to recognize and honor the spiritual depth of David's act of worship. In chastising David, Michal not only diminishes the value of sincere devotion to God but also reveals a disconnect from recognizing and valuing God's hand upon David's life. Her reaction, intended to chastise, instead starkly illustrates the manifestation of spiritual estrangement within the intimate weave of marital bonds.

Michal's oversight of the intrinsic value of respect and reverence for the anointing of God underscores a vital marital principle: respect extends beyond the mere acknowledgment of one's spouse to encompass a deep honor for the spiritual mantle they bear. Michal's indifference towards David's spiritual fervor not only signifies a personal rift but also signifies a broader detachment from the spiritual verities that shaped David's reign and destiny, reminding us of the imperative for shared spiritual values and a mutual celebration of God's work in our lives and marriages.

Identifying Michal-like Traits in Modern Relationships

In modern relationships, discerning Michal-like traits demand a keen eye for attitudes and behaviors that elevate worldly acclaim and material achievements above the essence of faith and spiritual depth. A 'Michal' in contemporary settings may present an outward facade of godly obedience. Yet, internally, they might harbor a subtle disdain or indifference towards authentic spiritual commitments and expressions of faith.

This discrepancy often reveals itself through a hesitance to engage in spiritual practices, outright criticism of such commitments, or a pronounced emphasis on social prestige and material wealth over the virtues of humility, service, and obedience to God.

Recognizing these traits in a potential partner is pivotal for those who yearn for a relationship rooted in shared spiritual values. It necessitates an introspective examination of a person's core values, response to acts of faith, and respect for godly vocations that might not conform to the worldly benchmarks of success and honor. This process transcends judgment; it is about identifying compatibility in the spiritual bedrock that constitutes a godly union.

The scriptures advocate for believers to be equally yoked (2 Corinthians 6:14), underscoring not just a shared profession of faith but a lived experience of faith, highlighting the need for a partner who respects, supports, and partakes in one's spiritual journey. The story of Michal and David acts as a beacon, urging us to select partners who not just honor our spiritual commitments but resonate with them, ensuring the most intimate of human connections mirror and honor the profound depths of our allegiance to God.

Amidst this backdrop of discernment and spiritual alignment, the story of Dick and Valerie unfolds, mirroring the ancient tale of Michal and David in a contemporary setting. Dick, akin to David, is a man of unwavering faith, his life a testament to devotion and service to God. Valerie attracted to Dick's vibrant spirit and passion, initially finds his spiritual fervor to be a complement to their union. However, as their paths diverge from the carefree days of youth into the complexities of adult life, the foundation of their relationship faces its crucible.

The scriptures come alive in 2 Samuel 6:14-22, offering a vivid tableau of spiritual celebration, with David's uninhibited dance before the Lord as its centerpiece. This expression of pure devotion starkly contrasts Michal's scornful perspective, a poignant reminder of the rift that can form when spiritual values diverge within a union. Dick's commitment to a missionary journey, an act mirroring David's unreserved worship, becomes a flashpoint for Valerie, revealing a chasm in their spiritual understandings and aspirations.

Valerie's reaction, a blend of incredulity and concern, echoes Michal's disdain, underscoring the challenges couples face navigating the delicate interplay of love, faith, and individual callings. Their story, set against the backdrop of modernity, invites us to reflect on the enduring importance of spiritual harmony in relationships, urging us to seek not just a partner but a fellow pilgrim on the journey of faith.

The Dangers of Marrying a Michal

Choosing a wife who mirrors Michal's indifference towards spiritual depth invites a cascade of challenges that extend beyond mere interpersonal discord. This choice can imperil the foundational pillars of one's faith, leading to a gradual but significant divergence from core spiritual beliefs and practices. Such relationships often exert subtle yet persistent pressures to sideline spiritual commitments in favor of conforming to a secular lifestyle, diluting the essence of one's calling and purpose.

While the Bible doesn't avoid addressing the complexities of spiritual harmony in marriage, it firmly warns against alliances that could dilute one's faith. The overarching biblical narrative emphasizes a marriage rooted in mutual spiritual respect and dedication. This scriptural wisdom isn't merely preventative but prescriptive, aiming to foster relationships that bolster rather than burden one's ministry.

Proverbs 4:23's counsel to guard one's heart speaks volumes about the intrinsic value of maintaining spiritual integrity. A relationship with a person who lacks a genuine commitment to faith can lead to compromises that stray from God's intended path, affecting the individual and the spiritual legacy left for future generations. It's a dynamic that questions the personal and communal aspects of faith, underscoring the importance of a wife who champions rather than challenges your ministry and convictions.

The ramifications of such a union are profound, touching on every facet of spiritual life, from personal devotion to communal service. A wife dismissive of spiritual values can inadvertently undermine your role and effectiveness within the church, fostering an environment of tension rather than mutual growth and support. This hampers a man of God's development and detracts from the couple's collective witness to the transformative power of faith.

Thus, scripture's guidance transcends mere caution, urging a deep, discerning look at a potential partner's spiritual character. It's a call to seek not just compatibility but a shared zeal for God's Kingdom, ensuring that the marriage becomes a conduit for mutual spiritual enrichment and a testament to God's enduring presence in our lives.

In essence, the decision to marry should be approached with a heart tuned to God's wisdom, seeking a partner whose life reflects a shared dedication to living out one's faith. It's a journey that demands more than compatibility checks—it requires a commitment to a shared spiritual vision, one that elevates the divine calling at the heart of the marital covenant.

Navigating Relationship Choices with Divine Wisdom

To steer clear of relationships that mirror the spiritually discordant nature of Michal's interaction with David, it's essential to embrace a blend of godly wisdom and proactive strategies. The scriptures offer a beacon of light for those seeking to align their relationship choices with God's will, ensuring a partnership that flourishes in shared faith and mutual respect for each other's spiritual journey.

Engaging in Prayerful Reflection: Prayer serves as the bedrock of discernment, offering a direct conduit to seeking God's wisdom and direction in choosing a partner. The admonition in Philippians 4:6-7 to bring our desires and concerns to God underscores the peace and clarity that comes from entrusting our relationship decisions to Him. Through prayer, individuals can gain insights into a potential spouse's spiritual alignment and character.

Wisdom Through Godly Insight: The biblical principle highlighted in Proverbs 15:22 about the value of multiple advisers reinforces the importance of seeking wisdom from those who walk in spiritual maturity. Consulting with mentors, pastoral leaders, or trusted Christian friends can provide objective advice and support, helping to illuminate God's path in pursuing a godly partner.

Scriptural Illumination for Decision-Making: Scripture is the ultimate guide for life's decisions, offering principles for wise living and relationships. Verses like 2 Corinthians 6:14 and Proverbs 4:23 serve as vital reminders of the importance of spiritual compatibility and the protection of one's heart. Immersing oneself in the Word aids in developing the discernment needed to identify traits that could undermine a spiritually harmonious marriage.

Cultivating a Heart of Discernment: Developing spiritual discernment is key to understanding God's perspective and making choices that reflect His desires for our lives. This involves an attunement to the Holy Spirit's guidance, a keen awareness of relational red flags, and a commitment to aligning one's life and choices with the teachings of Christ. A disciplined spiritual life enriched by worship, Bible study, and obedience enhances the ability to navigate the complexities of relationships with godly wisdom.

By integrating these approaches into the fabric of their decision-making, individuals can confidently approach their search for a life partner guided by the principles of faith, wisdom, and a deep commitment to aligning their relationships with God's plan. This method ensures the safeguarding of one's spiritual well-being and fosters the foundation for a marriage that glorifies God and enriches both partners spiritually.

Takeaway

In concluding this chapter on the caution against rushing to marry a Michal, we are reminded of the profound spiritual truths embedded in her story and its significance for contemporary believers. Michal's narrative serves as a stark warning of the potential pitfalls of marrying someone who does not share or respect one's spiritual commitments and the calling God has placed upon one's life. Her disdain for David's worship highlights a critical aspect of marital relationships: the necessity of mutual respect, support, and understanding of each other's spiritual expressions and journeys.

The story of Michal and David underscores the importance of seeking a partner who values and participates in shared worship, understands the sacrifices and commitments required to serve God, and stands by your side, encouraging and uplifting your faith. This is the bedrock upon which a godly marriage is built, one that not only withstands the challenges of life but also thrives, bringing glory to God and serving as a testament to His grace and love.

For young men on the path to finding a life partner, Michal's story is a poignant reminder to prioritize spiritual compatibility and to seek a woman whose heart is aligned with God's. It calls for a deep reflection on one's values and a commitment to pursuing relationships rooted in shared faith and devotion. This pursuit is not just about avoiding the pitfalls represented by Michal but about actively seeking a partnership that embodies the fullness of God's design for marriage.

As you contemplate this journey, let scripture be your guide, prayer your compass, and the Holy Spirit your counselor. Remember, choosing a spouse is not just a matter of the heart but a decision that shapes your spiritual legacy and impacts God's kingdom. May the lessons from Michal's story inspire you to seek a partner who will dance alongside you in worship, support you in your spiritual battles, and build a life that reflects the beauty and faithfulness of God's love.

In the quest for a godly marriage, let the words of Proverbs 3:5-6 be a beacon of light: "Trust in the Lord with all your heart, and lean not on your own understanding; in all your ways submit to him, and he will make your paths straight." (NIV) May this scripture guide you toward a union that celebrates and honors God, ensuring your marriage reflects His perfect love and plan.

Epilogue

In the journey through the pages of this book, we've traversed the complex and often challenging terrain of choosing a life partner guided by the timeless wisdom of the Bible. Each chapter has unfolded biblical narratives that offer profound insights into the qualities and pitfalls to be mindful of when seeking a spouse.

From the cautionary tales of Amnon's lust and Ahab's spiritual waywardness to the reflections on modern-day entanglements with figures reminiscent of Potiphar's wife and Michal, this journey has been an invitation to deep reflection and discernment for believers standing at the crossroads of marriage.

The essence of this book is not merely to warn or guide but to illuminate the path toward a godly union that honors and reflects God's design for marriage. In a world where the sanctity of marriage is often clouded by fleeting passions and worldly standards, the biblical narratives discussed herein serve as beacons of light, illuminating the virtues of patience, integrity, spiritual compatibility, and mutual respect. These stories remind us that the marriage covenant is not just a societal contract but a sacred vow before God, a partnership designed to glorify Him, foster spiritual growth, and build a legacy of faith.

Choosing a life partner is one of the most significant decisions a person will make, with implications that echo into eternity. This decision should be approached with prayer, wisdom, and a heart attuned to God's leading.

The characters we've explored, from Delilah's seduction to Lot's wife's backward glance, serve as mirrors reflecting to us the consequences of choices made in isolation from God's guidance. They remind us that in seeking a spouse, our primary allegiance must be to God, seeking His kingdom first, trusting that all other things, including a partner who shares our faith and values, will be added unto us (Matthew 6:33).

This book has also touched on the importance of self-examination and spiritual readiness for marriage. It is crucial that individuals not only seek the right partner but also strive to be the right partner. This means cultivating a life of devotion, character, and commitment to God's Word and understanding that marriage is a ministry of love, sacrifice, and service. As we've seen through the examples of Joseph's integrity and Daniel's unwavering faith, the strength of our character and our commitment to God profoundly impact our relationships and the choices we make.

As we draw this journey to a close, let us carry forward the lessons learned with a heart open to God's leading. Let us be mindful of the traits that draw us closer to Him and those that lead us away. Let us seek relationships that honor God, characterized by love, respect, and a shared commitment to serving

Him. The pursuit of a godly marriage is a journey of faith, a step into the unknown, trusting that God, who knows the end from the beginning, will lead us to the partner He has prepared for us.

In this quest for a life partner, let us be guided by the wisdom of Proverbs 19:14, which reminds us that *"Houses and wealth are inherited from parents, but a prudent wife is from the Lord."* (NIV) May this wisdom inspire young men and women to seek God's face in their search for a spouse, trusting that His plans are to prosper us and not to harm us, plans to give us hope and a future (Jeremiah 29:11).

As we close this book and look forward to applying these truths to our lives, I invite you to join me in a declaration of faith and commitment to God's perfect will for our marital futures. This declaration is not just a conclusion to our readings but a proclamation of our trust in God's promises and a renouncement of any hindrance that stands in the way of His divine plan for us.

Declaration:

Today, I renounce every soul tie in the name of Jesus. I testify in the name of Jesus that His purpose concerning my future, marriage, and destiny shall stand. I abort any plans of the enemy to cause a delay in my marriage in the name of Jesus.

I declare by the divine authority that the Holy Spirit will bring me into contact with the one the Lord has chosen for me as a partner in the name of Jesus. I release myself from any family captivity in marriage in the name of Jesus.

> *In the name of Jesus, I renounce demonic influences that produce ungodly relationships, disrespect, criticism, revenge, self-centeredness, rejection, verbal attacks, embarrassment, emotional manipulation, mind games, and punishment.*
>
> *Any form of delay that will cause me not to be relevant in my marriage is destroyed. Any form of woman or man that will cause me to backslide and to move away from the promise of God concerning my life is blocked and arrested in the name of Jesus.*
>
> *Let the one you have destined for me be released and come to me now in the name of Jesus. I declare that every hindrance or barrier that will block my partner and me from meeting be removed in the name of Jesus. By the power of the Holy Spirit, let every demonic veil catch fire in the name of Jesus. I declare today that my divine partner is safe and secure for a godly marriage in the name of Jesus.*

This declaration stands as a testament to our belief in the power of God's Word and prayer. It reflects our commitment to trust in God's timing and plan for our lives, including the beautiful journey toward finding a godly spouse.

May your path to marriage be paved with prayer, patience, and unwavering trust in the One who writes the best love stories. And as you walk this path, remember always to love God first, for it is in loving Him that we learn to love others truly and deeply.

May the grace of our Lord Jesus Christ, the love of God, and the fellowship of the Holy Spirit be with you all as you embark on this sacred journey toward a godly marriage. Amen.

About the Author

Archbishop Nicholas Duncan-Williams, with over forty years of ministry, serves as the Presiding Archbishop and General Overseer of Action Chapel International (ACI), based in Accra, Ghana. He also oversees the United Denominations of Action Chapel International, which encompasses over 150 affiliate and branch churches across North America, Europe, Asia, and Africa.

As the Founder and Chairman of Nicholas Duncan-Williams Ministries (previously known as Prayer Summit International), he organizes prayer summits worldwide, fostering revival in global cities through collective and intercessory prayer, alongside providing training.

Archbishop Duncan-Williams, renowned for his profound anointing in prayer and intercession, is widely acknowledged as the "Apostle of Strategic Prayer" among Christian leaders. His ministry has extended to advising and influencing world leaders, earning him widespread respect and accreditation. Known affectionately as "Papa," his reach transcends the global and influential, touching the lives of everyday people with the same fervor and dedication.

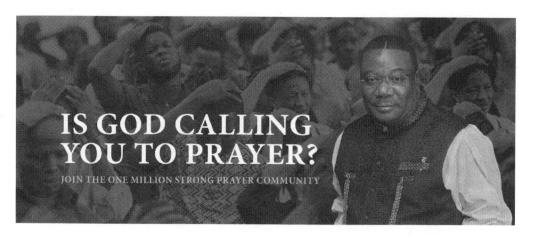

When you join One Million Strong, you will gain instant access to:

- **Financial Freedom Prayer Declaration**
- **Discover the Secrets to Effective Prayer** Course
- **Breakthrough in the Spiritual Realm** Audio

Made in the USA
Middletown, DE
08 July 2024

56915450R00082